THE
WELSH HIGHLAND
RAILWAY

Volume 3

• A PAST and PRESENT COMPANION •

Welsh Highland & Festiniog Railways.

VALE OF

BETTWS GARMON
Sheep Dog Trials

(£80 in Prizes), will be held at

YSTRAD FARM,

Friday & Saturday, Sept. 21st & 22nd, 1923,

On above dates Excursion Tickets will be issued to Bettws Garmon as under—

FROM.		Trains by which Tickets are issued.		3rd Class Fare.		Return trains leave Friday. at	Saturday.
		a.m.	a.m.	s.	d.	p.m.	p. m.
Bl. Festiniog	dept.	6 50	9 30	5	3	3 38	6 10
Tanygrisiau	...	6 58	9 37	4	11	3 38	6 10
Tanybwlch	...	7 18	9 54	4	3	3 38	6 10
Penrhyn	...	7 38	10 12	3	7	3 38	6 10
Minffordd	...	7 45	10 36	3	5	3 38	6 10
Portmadoc (New Station)		8 45	10 53	3	0	6 10	6 10
			P. M.				
Beddgelert	...	10 10	12 15	1	6	6 10	6 10 & 8 30
South Snowdon	...	10 50	1 0	0	10	6 10	6 10 & 8 30
Quellyn Lake	...	10 31	12 46	0	6	6 10	6 10 & 8 30
Bettws Garmon	arr.	11 14	1 26				
Tryfan Jct.	dept.	9 57	12 13	0	6	5 51	5 51
Dinas	...	9 45	12 0	0	10	5 51	5 51

Passengers from Festiniog Rly. Stations re-book at Portmadoc (New Station), and passengers joining the trains at Halts on the W. H. Rly. book to the nearest Station and there book Excursion Tickets to Bettws Garmon.

General Conditions governing the issue of Tickets at Reduced Fares

Children under 3 years of age free, 3 and under 12 half-fare.

The Company give notice that the tickets shewn in this Handbill are issued at reduced rate and are subject to the conditions that the Company shall not be liable for any loss, damage, injury or delay to passengers arising from any cause whatsoever.

Cheap Tickets are not transferable, and are available only on date of issue to and from the Stations mentioned upon them, and by the trains advertised, and if used to or from a Station beyond or short of the Station mentioned on the Tickets, or by trains not advertised, they will be forfeited and holders thereof will be charged the full ordinary fare for the whole distance travelled.

The Cheap Tickets will not be extended nor will any allowance be made on return portions not used. No Luggage allowed.

PORTMADOC Sept. 1923.

S. E. TYRWHITT, General Manager.

No 60   Jones & Co, Printers, Portmadoc.

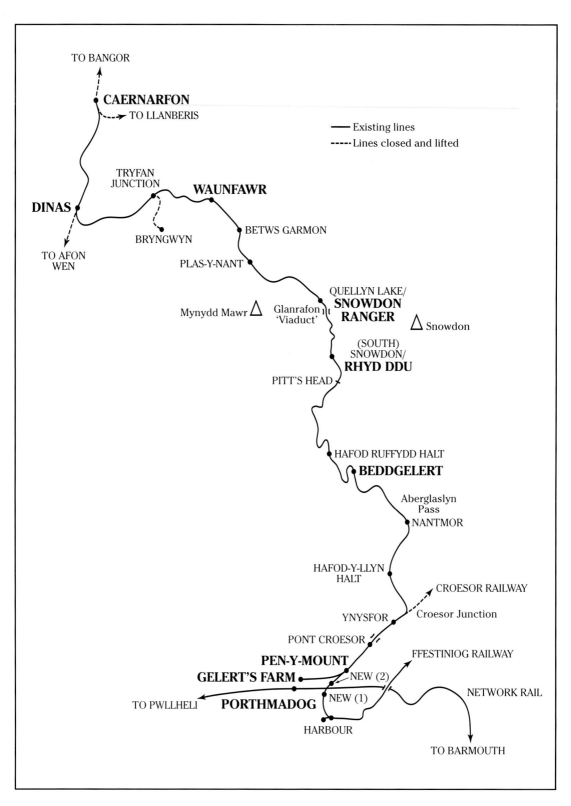

The Welsh Highland Railway and associated lines. Current WHR stations are shown in large type.

THE
WELSH HIGHLAND RAILWAY

Volume 3

· A PAST AND PRESENT COMPANION ·

Ain't no stoppin' us now!

John Stretton

· RAILWAY HERITAGE ·
from
The NOSTALGIA Collection

First published in 2009

British Library Cataloguing in Publication Data

A catalogue record for this book is available from the British Library.

ISBN 978 1 85895 259 8

Past & Present Publishing Ltd
The Trundle
Ringstead Road
Great Addington
Kettering
Northants NN14 4BW

Tel/Fax: 01536 330588
email: sales@nostalgiacollection.com
Website: www.nostalgiacollection.com

Printed and bound in the Czech Republic

All photographs credited 'MJS' were taken by the author.

Past and
Present

A Past & Present book
from
The NOSTALGIA *Collection*

ACKNOWLEDGEMENTS

As usual, I am indebted to a wide variety and number of people who have assisted in one way or another. Photographers, especially, have been very willing to submit images from their collections for consideration, and I am truly grateful to those who aided in this way – without them the book would have struggled to be born! They are duly credited throughout the collection, but I take this opportunity to offer all of them my profound gratitude. In addition, there are those who have helped me before and have been fool enough to put their name in the frame again! Among all of these, there are some who deserve especial mention and I would like to here present my sincere thanks to: John Keylock, for proofreading, patience and continual unflinching assistance; Dave Kent, for his time, courtesy and contribution; Tony Ellis, for his excellent selection of potential subtitles, including the winning selection; Mike Hart; Clare Britten; Roger Dimmick; John Wooden; Paul Lewin; David High; David Bateman; Adrian Gray; Tim Procter at the NRM; David Davies; Peter Rowlands; and Michelle Littleford (as she will always be to me!), for being there with encouragement and support. Finally, as usual, thanks goes to all at Silver Link Publishing – Peter for encouragement and for putting up with countless phone calls, David for his unflinching patience and courtesy, and to Mick and Will for their usual skilful and speedy editing and design. Thank you all!

CONTENTS

The restoration of the Welsh Highland Railway (WHR) has been overseen by the Ffestiniog Railway (FR). This 'joint partnership' has echoed the situation in the 1920s and 1930s, when, despite their diminutive size, FR locos, like terriers, ably fulfilled their duties between Porthmadog and Dinas Junction. In the summer of 1934 *Welsh Pony* stands at Beddgelert, ready to 'return to port', having run round its train. Though still extant in the 21st century, the loco is now a static exhibit, unlike its 'brothers' *Prince* and *Palmerston*. *F. M. Gates, WHR collection*

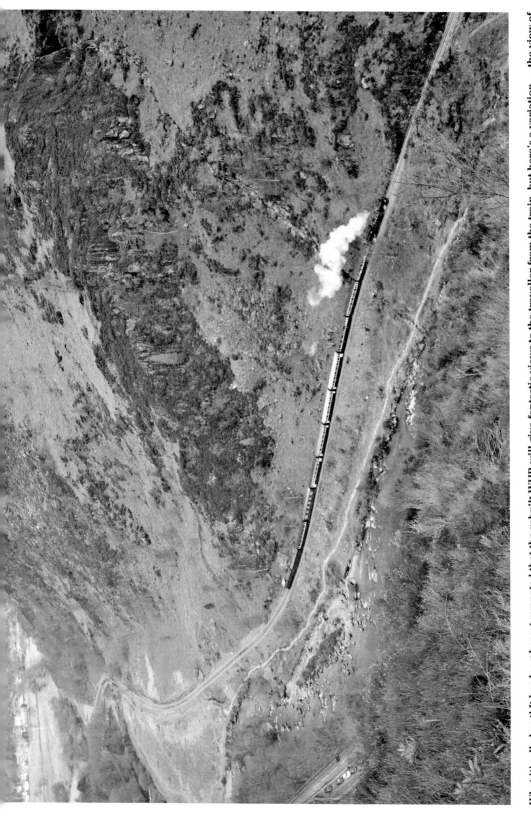

What it's all about! It has long been trumpeted that the rebuilt WHR will give fantastic views to the traveller from the train, but here's a variation … the view of the train. As if to herald the approach of a new era, the first day of spring, 21 March 2008, is the occasion for this test train as it heads towards the tunnels in the Aberglaslyn Pass – the first full-length train along the route for more than 70 years. The photographer has been rewarded for his efforts in climbing the mountainside with this mouth-watering view of Garratt No NG143 leading ten coaches. Funky diesel *Castell Caernarfon* is on the rear for insurance and 'ballast'.
Alasdair Stewart

INTRODUCTION

Welcome to the third in this trilogy looking at past views of the Welsh Highland Railway (WHR) and its rebuilding. It seems incredible to think that it is already more than a decade since the first short stretch of around 2½ miles, from Caernarfon to Dinas, opened to an excited public. Thereafter, the accretion of track mileage has progressed, slowly creeping ever onwards as the mix of contractors and volunteers pressed forward – an unstoppable force as dynamic and irresistible as the waves that confronted Canute! It has been unfailingly fascinating and inspirational to witness the transformation from what I first saw in 1989 to what is fast becoming the greatest achievement in 'heritage' railways in the world (at least in my opinion!).

As I am sure many will realise, the availability of previously unpublished photographs of the old WHR is somewhat limited. I have, as always, trawled widely in an attempt to find such gems but, bearing in mind the fact that the railway ceased operations in 1937 and that film and cameras were not what they are today, they are akin to the proverbial 'hen's teeth'! The mind boggles at what might have been captured for posterity if the digital age had been around then! However, I hope that even long-time avid aficionados will find some new delights on which to feast their eyes in this latest offering. With all this in mind, and the sheer scale of

As well as the Aberglaslyn Pass, the new WHR will delight and excite in equal measure as it courses through Snowdonia and the Beddgelert Forest, with many twists and turns and reverse curves. On 8 August 1935 *Russell* **is captured at the head of a northbound train as it negotiates its way through the foliage, with the imperious might of Snowdon in the distance.** *H. F. Wheeller, Roger Carpenter* collection

the rebuilding, I have devoted the final third of this volume to views of the construction and the work undertaken by contractors and volunteers. Mention should be made of all the contractors who have played their part, but in this Phase 4 development special credit goes to the G. H. James Cyf, who have battled and overcome many and various obstacles, natural and otherwise, to complete their piece of the jigsaw. Without all who 'went the extra mile' we would not be looking at a new railway from 2009.

I hope readers will enjoy the views of the various stages of development, but also derive some appreciation of the magnitude of the task. In terms of finance, matched funding and volunteer efforts, the costs of putting the WHR back on the map will see no change from £40 million – and largely because the 'real' railway is not like some glorified Hornby train set! There is far more to preparing the way for the eventual laying of rails – and initial preparation is most important in this task, as with any other worthwhile procedure – than merely clearing scrub or flattening a strip of land. There has been much expenditure on fencing, rights of way, culverts, drainage, etc. I have highlighted specific areas where appropriate in the captions and, again, I hope readers will be able to appreciate where large chunks of the overall budget have gone.

The worth of volunteers is recognised as 'matched funding' within grants, but their true value is in how much work they donate to the railway – before, during and after construction. I am only too pleased, therefore, to be able to pay tribute to them all, in whatever way they have assisted, and to dedicate the final third of the book to their efforts.

As those who are already familiar with my books will know, I derive huge pleasure in 'going back in time' and attempting to stand in the shoes of the original photographer. It is often not as easy as it might seem and, on so many occasions, I have been blessed with co-operation, guidance, hints, tips and information from many quarters, not least the members of the various railways that make up the WHR family, and their help is hereby readily acknowledged. Similarly, those who have helped with providing and/or checking information have been gracious with their time and expertise. Any mistakes are mine alone and, if any are found, I

Looking north, we have an unusual view of the Aberglaslyn Pass, the river and, above it, the two short tunnels on the railway trackbed. As seen on 5 October 1951, rails are absent and walkers have begun their meanderings along the trackbed and through the tunnels. Seemingly a 'permanent' scene, it is one that cannot now be easily recreated, however, due to the prolific spread of greenery over the intervening years. *Hugh Ballantyne*

would be grateful if they could be passed to the publisher, for I am keen that errors are not presented to or perpetuated by future historians.

The railway has achieved much in the last few years and, while there will now most likely be a period of consolidation and reflection, I am aware that the Directors, members and volunteers are already thinking about the next step. Much of the speed of this progress will be governed by the practical support of those keen to see developments – whether by finance or muscle – and one can pray that new, young volunteers will continue to join the railway and add their own brand of support. But all can do much by advertising the railway and its achievements, even if they are 'armchair' supporters. The Welsh Highland Railway is a special place with a potentially vital role to play in protecting the magnificent surroundings through which it runs. It would be wonderful to see the railway bringing people into the area, to enjoy its unique nature, without destroying that uniqueness through the influx of the motorcar!

The new WHR is one of the wonders of the railway world. I, for one, never thought I would see the reinstatement of the flat crossing with Network Rail's line into Porthmadog, or that the railway would be allowed to lay tracks across Britannia Bridge, on a road that is the artery into the town from the east. But it has happened, and I hope that this book will add to the appreciation of these and all the other achievements in completing the '26 miles of good road' – to slightly misquote one of Duane Eddy's records!

A competition was held for the subtitle to this third book – following 'A Phoenix Rising' and 'Halfway to Paradise'. The winner submitted around two dozen excellent suggestions and the final choice was a hard one, but the result is on the front cover. So, the railway has reached Porthmadog, has overcome many seemingly insurmountable obstacles, and is back in Harbour station, joining up again with the Ffestiniog Railway, as it did in the 1920s and '30s. A huge amount has been achieved, but there is more to come, for 'there ain't no stoppin' us now!'

We are fortunate that there were – and still are – skilful, dedicated and energetic photographers who thought nothing of travelling the length and breadth of the UK, capturing images on film. There may be more views of the railway 'out there'. I would be delighted to hear of any, especially from those who have not had their work previously published. Finally, by all means use this book as a sort of travel guide – go out and enjoy yourselves!

Here is a rural idyll that looks, to all intents and purposes, as if there had never been anything resembling a railway here. However, appearances are deceptive in this portrait of the old Beddgelert station in black and white – the same as the sheep! The base of the water tower still stands in July 1988, framing the animals with, just visible in the foreground, the loco inspection pit still providing a trap for the unwary! One white building in the village is just glimpsed between the trees, to the right of the tower upright. *Terry Gough*

'THE BOYS ARE BACK IN TOWN'
by Dave Kent
Chairman, Welsh Highland Railway Society

For those of you who have purchased the previous two editions of this series of books, it is difficult to imagine that a period of only 10 years has taken place between all three. In the first edition I mentioned how my father told stories of imaginary railways when I was young, and that was the way we felt when we started this project, that one had an imaginary idea of the completed line. As you read this, that project for the reconstruction of the Welsh Highland trackbed and its line is now complete, so your imagination of our railway is no longer required!

That the vista throughout the entire 25 miles of railway is always stunning, never repeated and always fresh to the eye is one reason why we have to thank the foresight of the Victorian speculators who built the first part of the line in the 1870s. Many people have been amazed at the views one can see on the existing line to Rhyd Ddu, and I am sure that as a traveller over the new section to Porthmadog you will also enjoy the spectacular scenery not accessible for the last 70 years. To the casual observer, the past decade of railway rebuilding has probably seemed to have made progress almost like a dream. Of course the reality of that achievement is the enormous amounts of work carried out by the many people, both paid and volunteers, which has resulted in the line you see now. It is only their determination – indeed, their vision of the complete railway – that has allowed the line to progress in such a way that we have been able to complete the rebuilding of this line in such a short time.

This close-up view of Single Fairlie 0-6-4T *Moel Tryfan* is undated, but is before 1923, when it was cut down to allow service over the FR, as noted on page 18 – compare the height of the chimney, dome and cab to the portrait on that page. Note also the sand drum on the front buffer beam – the fireman would hand-sand the rails from this rather precarious position. Health & Safety inspectors today would have heart attacks at the thought! *WHR Heritage Group collection, MJS collection*

When we started the project we were a collection of individuals with a common aim and a big imagination of the completed railway; as time has progressed we are now a very close-knit team who have turned the dream into reality. Working our way over the summit less than a mile from our temporary terminus at Rhyd Ddu, we started building the line down towards Cardigan Bay and Porthmadog. 'All down hill from here,' it was remarked. Well, maybe in terms of height above sea level it was, but in terms of the amount of work and its complexity we found that gravity played a powerful part in the proceedings and a lot of care was exercised over the next 5½ miles of line. Passing through Beddgelert Forest is a magical experience – not all trees and no views, but a changing landscape where the line twists and turns to show this delightful place at its best. The civil engineering and track formation in this area are some of the most challenging to a railway within the UK and cannot be found anywhere else, so as you travel this line it demonstrates just how unique it is.

Four tunnels and a wonderful rock shelf bring you beautiful views of the Glaslyn River and its gorge before we reach the peace and tranquillity of the Traeth Mawr with its long straights and gradual curves, and its wonderfully long-distance views, very different again from the Forest. As we approach Porthmadog we can give you another unique experience as we travel across the Cambrian Coast standard-gauge railway line, the only place in the UK where passenger trains of two different gauges cross each other on the level. Finally we arrive at Porthmadog Harbour station, having crossed the main A487 trunk road and a river bridge in one short stretch. At this point we join up with our sister line, the world-famous Ffestiniog Railway, but that, as they say, is another story.

In this series of books we hope you have gained a flavour of why the line is so special to so many of us, and why it just had to be rebuilt. Now that you have had a chance to come and ride the line, we hope you will understand and share our enthusiasm for its restoration. As Chairman of the supporters I extend a welcome to any and all of you who may be interested in this project, because although we have achieved an enormous amount so far by relaying the line, we now have to make our railway into the very best 2-foot-gauge line in the world.

Welcome to the Welsh Highland Railway, 25 miles long and so very different from anything else you have visited. Enjoy your trip, and we hope that we will see you again. Now, what was that about dreaming the impossible…?

Carriage stock is so often disregarded by the average enthusiast, with locomotives being far more popular, but they were and still are vital to the successful running of a passenger service. Over the years the designs on both the FR and WHR were numerous, and even so-called standard coaches could have their own idiosyncrasies! On 8 August 1935 Ashbury semi-open 'Summer Coach' No 24 stands at Dinas between duties. Inherited by the FR at the close of the 1936 season, it was renumbered 23 and in this guise still runs on the new WHR – a remarkable survivor! Note the minimal clearance between the running board and the ground, which, with the lack of top-quality maintenance on the trackbed in the 1920 and '30s, could have led to serious operational incidents. Note also the petrol pump on the right. *H. F. Wheeller, Roger Carpenter collection, MJS collection*

'THE LONG AND WINDING ROAD'
by John Keylock
Secretary and founder member of the WHR Heritage Group

The Welsh Highland Railway that closed in 1937 began its southbound journey at Dinas Junction, but the line that one rides today starts in Caernarfon, thus fulfilling a plan first devised in the 1870s. The section of the 'new' WHR between the terminus at Caernarfon and Dinas Junction is not without its historical association, for, being laid on the trackbed of the standard gauge branch that ran from Bangor, through Caernarfon to Afon Wen, it both parallels and incorporates the alignment of the Nantlle Railway, which opened in 1828 as a horse-drawn tramway, to carry slates from the quarries in the Nantlle Valley to the quayside at Caernarfon. However, it is the line between Dinas and Rhyd Ddu that retains many structures built by the North Wales Narrow Gauge Railway (NWNGR) for its complete opening in 1881. The station building and goods shed at Dinas are complete survivors from this period.

There are many bridges over and under roads built in the area's vernacular incorporating decorative yellow bricks. Where the line passes under a road, the trackbed has been lowered by the current railway – and the bridge underpinned – to accommodate, particularly, the ex-South African Garratt locomotives, which require a more generous loading gauge. Of the original dilapidated station buildings, that at Tryfan Junction is the most completely extant and a fund has long been established – by the WHR Heritage Group – for its eventual restoration. This scheme is high on the list of the Group's priorities. A branch originally ran from here to Bryngwyn, to bring down slates from the several quarries on Moel Tryfan mountain; indeed, this 'branch' was the NWNGR's main purpose and was considered the 'main line' at a time when the slate trade was at its peak. Sadly, this was very soon to be in decline.

At Waunfawr, the next station on from Tryfan Junction, there was originally a similar station building but, alas, it had to be dismantled to accommodate the 21st century railway. It is hoped that some of the salvaged materials will be used in the reconstruction of Tryfan Junction station. All that remains from the 'old days' is the Station Master's house, now much modified as the Snowdonia Parc pub, adjacent to the new station.

Immediately before the first crossing of the Afon Gwyrfai – by a modern replacement of the original bowstring bridge – are the remains of Betws Garmon station building. Semi-derelict, it is not intended to re-open this as a stopping place. From here a feeder line came in from nearby Hafod-y-Wern quarry. On the slopes of Moel Eilio, a little to the south of the station site, is an outstanding series of adits, from which much iron ore was extracted during the First World War.

Entering Nant y Betws, the railway keeps close company with the Afon Gwyrfai, crossing it near Salem – where the old WHR established a halt – and at Plas y Nant. Both of these bridges are original NWNGR structures. Today's halt at this latter location was part funded by the Heritage Group. Continuing south towards Rhyd Ddu, the line soon looks down on Quellyn Lake before arriving at Snowdon Ranger, where the station building has been in private ownership since the 1960s, and a completely new facility has been provided for today's WHR.

The next prominent feature is a girder bridge spanning a deep ravine, down which tumbles the Afon Trewewnydd on its way to that same Quellyn Lake. Immediately afterwards is the site of Glanrafon Sidings, to which an incline from the adjacent hillside brought slate for transportation to Dinas and on to Caernarfon. This was the most important quarry on this

Above A view of an England engine and three carriages that, happily, will now be capable of recreation. With the Afon Glaslyn out of sight at the foot of this view, *Welsh Pony* is seen again, climbing north through the Aberglaslyn Pass in 1934, with coaches 27 and 26 and an FR bogie brake bringing up the rear. *Brian Jones, WHR Heritage Group collection*

Below Much photographed in earlier times, and increasingly since reinstatement, was the flat crossing with the erstwhile Cambrian Railways line. Much rarer is a view of the nearby foot crossing, seen from a train that has just passed over it on 8 August 1935, looking back towards the standard gauge station in Porthmadog. In the present century this is now the access point to the site of WHR Ltd, otherwise known as Gelert's Farm. Note the two ladies standing outside the crossing cottage, shading their eyes to watch the passage of the train. *H. F. Wheeller, Roger Carpenter collection*

stretch of the line, with the owners in the late 1870s helping to finance the NWNGR so they could speed up the transfer of their product to the market place. Still extant are the remains of the 'weighhouse', although it remains uncertain that there was ever a weighbridge adjacent. From here the line twists and turns in its progress to the village of Rhyd Ddu, around 12 miles from Caernarfon and 627 feet above sea level, where the original station was on the site of today's toilet block and overflow car park!

Apart from the section of line from Rhyd Ddu to Hafod Ruffyd – which was laid in 1908 – the journey from Rhyd Ddu to Porthmadog is on a formation finalised with the coming of the WHR in 1923. Sir Robert McAlpine's price for this construction contract was £60,819 – or approximately £5,000 per mile. Compare this with the 21st-century cost of £1 million per mile! So what did the contract involve?

Working from north to south, the 1908 section was relaid on an improved base between Pitt's Head and Pont Cae'r Gors. From Ty'n y Coed, in the Beddgelert Forest, to just north of the Beddgelert station site the route was realigned on a new formation incorporating loops to provide easier gradients more compatible with steam locomotive operation. Then, beyond the Goat Tunnel, immediately to the south of Beddgelert station, a new route was engineered to cross the Afon Glaslyn at Bryn-y-Felin and bring the line to the head of the Aberglaslyn Pass and onto the trackbed created between 1904 and 1906.

The tunnels in the Pass were virtually ready to use. Much of the formation between the southern end of the long tunnel and a junction with the Croesor Tramway had been determined and, apart from having to cross two rivers, the 'going' would have been reasonably straightforward. Onwards from Croesor Junction, it was a case of upgrading the Croesor Tramway and making a connection with the Ffestiniog Railway at Harbour station. The last section, from south of the Cambrian crossing to Harbour station, was financed by the FR. Included in the overall price was the cost of upgrading the NWNGR section from Dinas to Rhyd Ddu.

Over a century has passed since those first practical attempts to connect Rhyd Ddu with Porthmadog, thus linking Caernarfon to the southern seaport. Today's reconstructed WHR therefore represents the fulfilment of an even earlier, 1870s ambition. The passage of time has fortunately not erased many of those century-old construction features, so again travelling south from Rhyd Ddu it is worth reflecting on what remains of the railway's heritage.

At Pitt's Head the line is crossed by a road bridge built by the Porthmadog, Beddgelert & South Snowdon Railway in 1908; immediately afterwards are the piers of an uncompleted overbridge originally intended for livestock to cross the railway. The summit of the line is just before Pont Cae'r Gors and construction south was by cutting an embankment as far as Coed Mawr loop. Between Ty'n y Coed and Cwm Cloch Isaf is a deep cutting on a 1 in 28 gradient, a positive relic of the PB&SSR's intention to use electric traction! There are remains of a PB&SSR accommodation bridge where this route meets today's alignment; and in the throat of Beddgelert station three similar bridges span the access road to Cwm Cloch, the Afon Cwm Cloch and a footpath. To meet modern needs, these have been modified.

Beyond Beddgelert station are the Goat cutting and tunnel, and almost immediately beyond the tunnel a spur swings left to approach the bridge spanning the Beddgelert to Porthmadog road – this would have carried the line of rail to a different crossing of the Afon Glaslyn, closer to Beddgelert than that actually provided at Bryn y Felin. The twin parapets for the earlier intended route can still be seen standing proud in the adjacent field! The tunnels in the spectacular Aberglaslyn Pass are a fitting memorial to Edwardian civil engineering skills. Immediately south of the long tunnel are bridges over the access lane to Cwm Bychan and the Afon Cwm Bychan.

After Nantmor cutting and embankment there is little of significance until Croesor Junction is reached, 8.7 miles from Rhyd Ddu. From here the WHR utilised the trackbed of the 1864 Croesor Tramway, whose major engineering feature was the bridge across the Afon Glaslyn, illogically named 'Pont Croesor'. The supporting piers of the railway bridge have proved their status after all this time and have been reused to carry the new railway across the river.

Just before reaching Cae Pawb, the flat crossing with Network Rail's Cambrian Coast line, there is a junction with the WHR's Porthmadog 'Gelert's Farm' operation, based on the original slate transhipment sidings. The Cambrian crossing now has a replica signal box and protective gates on the narrow gauge. Immediately beyond is the site of the 1923 Portmadoc (sic) station, of which all that remains is the concrete support of the water tower, which mirrors that at Beddgelert. Then looming large on the left is the Flour Mill, before the railway threads its way behind the town, on to Britannia Bridge and into the FR's Harbour station.

Thus, despite the passage of more than 100 years, there is much that remains to be seen and appreciated and, with plans for a narrow gauge museum at Gelert's Farm, it is hoped that more artefacts from the original railways can be displayed. The new WHR hopes and trusts that visitors will seek out and appreciate some of the delights outlined above; after all, Porthmadog was the cradle of the narrow gauge worldwide, and the original Festiniog and Welsh Highland Railways were outstanding achievements.

14

CAERNARFON TO RHYD DDU

While it is not the norm for your author to re-use images, he makes no apologies for revisiting this view of the railway alignment at Caernarfon, adjacent to the Castle. In the early years of the 20th century a passenger train for Llanberis emerges from the tunnel that has brought the train from Bangor to this point. To the left, the tall ships and the railway are combining to load and unload the vast amounts of slate, freight and goods that gave added importance to the town.

A century later the vista is vastly changed. The castle and some of its neighbouring buildings still stand, but the railway has been swept clear of both quayside and what remains of the tunnel, which can be seen at the far end of the tall right-hand wall. Happily, however, as viewed from the footbridge to the houses (above right) on 15 April 2008, a railway has returned to the site. Opening on 12 October 1997, the new Welsh Highland Railway has since developed and improved its presence at this northern terminus, with car parking, toilets and a bookshop all in place for visitors and/or intending travellers. *Dave Southern collection/MJS*

Facilities have also been installed at Caernarfon for the locomotives, in the form of a capacious water tank. This also gives the waiting public the opportunity to witness another aspect of operating a railway. On 16 September 2000, those present were certainly treated to a rare sight of three locomotives at this station. At the head of the train on the left, two of the railway's ex-Beyer Peacock Garratts – Nos 138 and 143 – await the 'right away' to haul the 1130 departure for Waunfawr, while on the right *Russell*, built in 1906 and the sole surviving locomotive from the original North Wales Narrow Gauge Railway (NWNGR)/Welsh Highland Railway, is on display, having had its thirst quenched!

The current railway is also home to yet another 'ancient'! Built in 1909 at Manchester's Beyer Peacock works for service in Tasmania, No K1 was repatriated to the UK more than half a century later, having last worked in 1929! The world's first locomotive built to Henry Garratt's groundbreaking and, at the time, unique design, it has been lovingly restored, initially by enthusiasts and, more recently, overseen by the Ffestiniog Railway. After early teething troubles, it gave its first public run to Rhyd Ddu on 8 September 2006. It is seen here at Caernarfon, in spotless condition and complete with Tasmanian and Welsh flags, shortly before that historic return to service. *Both MJS*

A little over 2½ miles from Caernarfon, Dinas Junction was the first stop on the mostly single-line LNWR/LMS standard-gauge line to Afon Wen, as well as the northern terminus of the NWNGR/WHR route from Portmadoc (as it was then spelled). In 1911 the standard-gauge side is enjoying a moment of full employment, as a six-coach train waits to leave for Bangor on the left while what is thought to be one of Webb's 'Cauliflower' 0-6-0 passenger locos pauses with a rake of seven distinctly varied carriages bound for Afon Wen. The driver of the latter and a member of the station staff are conversing with the smartly dressed lady on the platform. The narrow-gauge WHR tracks are to the right, with the timber-built waiting room squat on the platform. The exchange sidings between the two gauges can be seen in the distance, above the locomotive.

The site at Dinas has seen much change over the past century, not least following the closure to traffic in the 1960s and conversion into a Council yard, full of building materials, after the rails had been lifted. Happily, however, both the stone station building and adjacent goods shed have survived, complete with trademark yellow edging bricks. Views of the various transitions – and fascinating detail differences – can be seen on pages 92-93 of Volume 1, and make interesting comparisons with this more recent portrait from 8 September 2006. In the early-afternoon sunshine, *Castell Caernarfon* stands in the down platform shortly before resuming its run to Rhyd Ddu, the southern terminus at the time. *LNWR, WHR collection/MJS*

At the narrow-gauge WHR side of Dinas Junction station, with the tiny standard-gauge waiting shelter visible on the left, Single Fairlie *Moel Tryfan* stands with its mixed rake of FR carriage and wagons forming the 1245 service to Portmadoc on 3 April 1926. Supplied by the Vulcan Foundry at Newton-le-Willows in 1875 together with sister loco *Snowdon Ranger*, the articulated 0-6-4T survived until the end of the WHR in the mid-1930s, utilising the frames of *Snowdon Ranger* along the way in 1917. In 1923 it was cut down in height to enable it to work over FR metals, and the reduced cab and chimney are clear from this view.

It is hard to imagine that this view was taken from the same vantage point, but indeed it is! On 8 September 2006 the results of nigh on ten years of development and improvement by the restorationists are plain to see, both in the rearranged layout and the clean lines of the new station. The station building survives – its roof can just be seen above the coach in the 'past' view – and has been renovated to award-winning standards and converted to present-day use by the new railway. *Ken Nunn, MJS collection/MJS*

Both these NWNGR locomotives were named after famous people. James Cholmeley Russell was a wealthy and canny lawyer who was elected chairman of the NWNGR's board in June 1879. Ironically, in 1904 he was also the railway's Receiver and it is perhaps not surprising, therefore, that the locomotive built in 1906 for the railway came to be named after him. Seen by the signal box at Dinas on 23 June 1909, *Russell* is in company with the slightly younger *Gowrie*.

The rather complicatedly designed 0-6-4T *Gowrie* was new in 1908 and named some time before this view in Dinas yard, prior to a run south with a rake of loaded wagons. As Gowrie Colquhoun Aitchison succeeded J. C. Russell as Receiver of the NWNGR, it is presumed that the 'tradition' set by *Russell* was followed by his successor, possibly around 1909, as the loco appears to have a nameplate in the upper view, but certainly before 1912 when J. C. Russell died. The railway's representatives here do not look over-pleased at having their portrait taken! *Ken Nunn Collection, LCGB/G. M. Perkins, WHR collection*

Russell is seen again, in August 1936, but this time in post-1923 cut-down state. Willie Hugh Williams, the driver, and what appears to be a visitor pose for their portraits, with an LMS train to the left and *Russell* seemingly anxious to be off! Compare the views of the loco here and in the upper picture on the previous page and the alterations are obvious. As well as the cut-down chimney, dome and cab, the buffer bucket has been enlarged, the sandbox atop the boiler has been repositioned and the vacuum pump removed from the tank front.

Once more the transformation is dramatic! *Russell* was standing roughly where the right-hand white groundsheet lies in this view. It is 8 September 2006 and Gala preparations are under way for what would turn out to be a 'Superpower Weekend' blessed with blue skies and warm sunshine. The scene is quiet at this point, but would be much livelier ere long! *W. H. Whitworth, WHR collection/MJS*

This slightly different aspect of *Russell* dates from 1935. Running round its train, with the fireman ready to dismount to couple up the coaches, this broadside view shows it passing the Station Master's house at Dinas. Considering the length of journeys being undertaken, there is precious little room within the guardrails atop the firebox to contain the vital coal supplies! Note how this view also displays the convoluted valve gear.

The house still stands, but is now protected by an established hedge and its windows have been replaced within the attractive (now painted) edging bricks. Tracks no longer run here, replaced by tarmac and wheels of a different sort. On 8 September 2006 a garden has been started on the railway land in the foreground and a new dwelling has sprung up in the background. *H. B. Tours, Martin Cook collection, MJS collection/MJS*

In earlier times, the entrance to Dinas Junction station was by way of steep footpaths to the two standard-gauge tracks from the road overbridge immediately to the south of the station. As the NWNGR/WHR line left the station, passing the Station Master's house and running under the road bridge, it passed carriage sheds, then curved sharply eastwards to run past the engine shed and signal box. These latter two are to the right of this undated view, with the standard-gauge line out of sight further to the right.

The Council replaced the sheds with new buildings and the resultant layout is seen on 8 September 2006. The old engine shed can still be seen at the far end, and the line still curves past this, but now from the direction of the standard-gauge approach, to the right, due to the aforementioned tarmac covering of the original route. The church spire is just visible in both shots. *Photomatic, WHR collection/MJS*

Down on the ground beyond the bridge we can see the separation of the gauges and the fence dividing them as the two lines head south from Dinas Junction station. In 1942, with the carriage sheds to the right, the railway's coaching stock is on view for the benefit of potential purchasers. Note the two styles of bridge, with the much earlier one over the WHR of much more traditional design and much lower over the tracks than its neighbour over the LMS route.

In this dramatic transformation only the two bridges (with the standard-gauge one showing signs of more recent rebuilding compared to the 'past' view) confirm that this is indeed the same vantage point. The current railway's transition from the standard-gauge to the narrow-gauge trackbed is more clearly seen from this angle, on 8 September 2006, with the old narrow-gauge trackbed subsumed beneath the aforementioned tarmac. *A. E. Rimmer, WHR collection/MJS*

Ah, the days when small boys wanted to be train drivers! Looking towards Dinas Junction on 1 June 1934, four young tykes enjoy a rare moment of being up close and personal with *Moel Tryfan* outside the carriage shed, accompanied by a man in waistcoat and flat cap. Driver Goronwy Roberts stands on the footplate, ensuring that the loco remains static! More than 70 years later, one wonders if any of the lads are still alive and, if so, 'where are they now?'.

The bridge survives, complete with tell-tale yellow bricks, but all around is change. On 8 September 2006, the present sheds are further from the road and, as already seen, tarmac and motor cars have replaced rails and steam engines. The trees and other greenery have greatly benefited over the years, with hedge and trees hiding the old goods shed, which still stands, beyond the distant car. *G. E. Hughes, WHR collection/MJS*

If you can't beat them, join them! Accompanying their husbands during a visit to the closed WHR in October 1941, inspecting the line and witnessing some of the rail reclamation, Mrs Bolton and Mrs Boyd-Carpenter take a temporary seat in an old slate wagon outside the carriage shed at Dinas. That the railway has been closed some four years at this time is evidenced by the rapid colonisation of the trackbed by grass and the absence of doors to the shed.

The replacement shed now occupied by the current railway is a far more substantial affair and now acts as accommodation for the railway's loco stock. As seen on 8 September 2006, progress by the restorationists over the previous decade has been equally substantial, not only on the ground but also with the locomotives being operated. History is being made here, as the first and very last Garratt to be built by Beyer Peacock stand side-by-side outside the shed. On the left is No K1 of 1909, being prepared for its first passenger run since restoration, with ex-South African Railways No NG143 (of 1958) displaying the advances in design and size over the years. *WHR Heritage Group collection/MJS*

In this view from 1942, one of the rail reclamation trains is passing Tryfan Junction station. Still in one piece here – but now without its nameboard above the doorway and the telegraph pole close to the door – the station building was to become swallowed by bushes and trees over the years following the lifting of the rails (see page 20 of Volume 1) and to succumb to the ravages of time and undergrowth by losing its roof and much of its upper walls. The Simplex tractor hauling the train makes its way towards Dinas and unloading.

The bushes and trees have been cleared and the current state of the building is revealed. Happily it has been 'adopted' by the Heritage Group of the WHR and will hopefully eventually regain its former glory. However, situated on a fairly steep gradient – up from Dinas – and in the wilds, with no buildings nearby and narrow and tortuous road access, it is unlikely to re-open to passengers in the foreseeable future. It will, nevertheless, together with the Bryngwyn branch 'slate trail', provide an additional point of interest for the traveller. *A. E. Rimmer, WHR collection/MJS*

After Dinas Junction, Waunfawr became the next temporary terminus as the rebuilt railway pushed southwards. Like Tryfan Junction, the old station building was to suffer the attentions of time and weather, leading to the state seen here on 23 September 1958. The single line between stations was augmented here by a passing loop, but with just one ground-level platform face, immediately to the right of the building in this view. The track once curved towards the right-hand distant tree, passing a signal box, and in earlier times there was even a siding running behind the station building.

This is the same scene but from the road overbridge. The station building stood roughly where the left-hand track meets the new platform end, and the original intention was to rebuild the structure on the new platform surface. However, although the bricks and stones of the facility were numbered, they mysteriously disappeared during the creation of the new site and the possibility was lost! On 26 January 2008 the present island platform has its footbridge in place and flower beds adorn the area, but the proposed waiting shelter is still to be provided. To the right stands Tafarn Snowdonia Parc Brewpub & Campsite, with its children's playground strategically placed to watch the trains. A large car park serves both pub and railway and many travellers have enjoyed meals and drinks here between rail journeys. *MJS collection/MJS*

Like Tryfan Junction and Waunfawr, Betws Garmon station building is but a shadow of its former self. There are currently no plans to renovate this and it will remain as a testament to what legacy was left to the restorationists by way of buildings. The structure, which still stands undisturbed off to the left of this view, is close by the Afon Gwyrfai, and the original bowstring bridge can be seen crossing the waters on 6 April 1977, with the site of Garreg Fawr Slate Quarry on the hill beyond.

Sadly, it was discovered that the old bridge was in no state to carry the much greater bulk and weight of the Garratts that would be hauling the new trains. After much searching, an appropriate structure was found in Rotherham, surplus to Network Rail's requirements. As a skew bridge, it needed its ends 'trimmed' to straighten it for use at Betws Garmon and this was done with just millimetres to spare – the river had scoured its banks and attacked the former bridge abutments, leading to a wider span. The cost of purchase, transportation and re-profiling was met by the Welsh Highland Society. The bridge is seen in place on 26 January 2008. *Ray Ruffell, Silver Link Publishing collection/MJS*

In this view of the bridge over the Afon Gwyrfai, Betws Garmon station building is behind the photographer and we are looking towards the eponymous village. Viewed on 15 April 1963, rails have been absent for more than 20 years and both trackbed and bridge have been left to the mercies of wind and weather. The bridge in the distance carries the A4085 Caernarfon to Beddgelert road over the railway. Note how the mist is blindfolding the mountain to the right.

   The view on 26 January 2008 shows the new WHR line in place and improvements on and around the railway. The new bridge and its new abutments share the foreground, with the renovated flood relief culvert just beyond and the relatively new road bridge in the distance. At an oblique angle to the railway, this A4085 bridge causes the tracks to deviate from the straight as they pass underneath. Sans mist, the mountain on the right can now be seen. Note the guard rails over the bridge. *Gerald Baxter, MJS collection/MJS*

One could be forgiven for thinking this is a model – and, indeed, it would make a superb blueprint for one – but it is the real thing. In an undated view, probably from the 1920s, the edge of the village of Salem is to the left and the road passing the entrance to Plas y Nant, prior to the Lodge being built, is top centre. The site of Plas y Nant Halt was around the curve, top right. The diminutive footbridge on the left spans the outflow of an early reservoir for the Caernarfon Water Board, fed by the Afon Gwyrfai, which approaches the railway over a weir immediately to the right of the pool in this view. *John Keylock collection*

We are looking towards Snowdon's majestic peak, the delightfully rural scene seemingly providing no evidence of there ever having been a railway here. However, peering over the parapet of the A4085 road bridge at Castell Cidwm in the early 1970s, the trackbed emerges from the proliferation of greenery and runs, arrow-like, into the distance. See also the views on page 55 of Volume 2.

The railway is very close to the underlying water table as it passes under the road bridge and drainage has been a problem in the rebuilding and will no doubt continue to be so if the heavy rains of the 21st century continue. It is to be hoped that the waters will not cancel too many trains, but they do add to the sights that can be enjoyed along the route! As seen on 8 September 2006, the new railway makes a fine sight as it strikes towards Snowdon, here visible to all, without the cloud that so often shrouds the mountain top. *Jon Marsh, MJS collection/MJS*

Above Shortly after Castell Cidwm, the railway climbs the flank of the surrounding hills and the traveller is granted views of the A4085 running alongside the extensive waters of Llyn Cwellyn (Quellyn Lake). The sheet of water is bounded by mountainsides, as seen to the left of this view, as Goronwy Roberts momentarily peers back along his train some time in 1936, driving *Russell* bunker-first on the return run from Beddgelert to Dinas. *H. B. Tours, MJS collection*

Below On 8 August 1935 a boisterous crowd of Scouts enjoy a trip along the line, thought to be somewhere in the same area; some of them could be looking at the lake, as they appear to be taking advantage of the excellent viewing opportunities granted by the numerous windows. *H. F. Wheeller, Roger Carpenter collection*

While what was known as Phase 4 – the rebuilding from Rhyd Ddu to Porthmadog – was in progress, the former station acted as terminus, almost exactly halfway between Caernarfon and the line's southern goal. With the original trackbed into Rhyd Ddu – or South Snowdon as it was also known – taken over by the National Park for parking, the new railway was forced to devise an alternative. The solution entailed buying some of the adjacent farmland for the actual station site and blasting a path through large rocks on the approach. On 20 October 2001 this process is under way, with the new cutting directly beyond the fence post. 'Work in progress' is the description at this point, with piles of steel sleepers in the foreground awaiting future use.

With the work complete, track laid and new fencing in place to protect foot and road access to the foot of Snowdon to the right, the view looks very different. With the remains of the original trackbed though the left-hand gate, No K1 steams into the station on 7 September 2008 with the 1045 Caernarfon-Rhyd Ddu service. Note that it again bears the Tasmanian and Welsh flags, as it did two years earlier on its first runs, but that the weather conditions are the opposite of what was enjoyed on that earlier occasion! *Both MJS*

There is no mistaking on which railway we are travelling! This is the roadside view of Rhyd Ddu station buildings, then with a South Snowdon nameboard, but no more trains will be arriving here as the date is May 1939 and the railway had ceased operations two years earlier. Consequently, the tiny parking space is unlikely to see many vehicles and the rather hopeful 'Parking Ground, Motor Cars 1/-' notice will no longer be an earner for the railway!

It is dubious whether the wall in the bottom right-hand corner of the 'past' view is the same as in the present-day view, especially as the former was mostly made up of slate rather than stone. Therefore a slightly wider aspect has been taken, to show the present-day building that houses public toilets, and which has the original trackbed running in front of it covered in tarmac. On 26 January 2008 the new platform can just be glimpsed to the right of the toilet block. *Photomatic, MJS collection/MJS*

34

RHYD DDU TO BEDDGELERT

With the railway successfully operating to Rhyd Ddu from Caernarfon, the next stage was to push south and progress Phase 4. With the station and village of Rhyd Ddu in the middle distance, this view on a bright 17 October 2005 shows the preparation of the trackbed onwards towards Pitt's Head (behind the camera), with ballast laid part way but still in need of further attention. While the railway formation is still in its early stages, a degree of smoothing will be needed before the ballast and track are laid and tamped prior to opening, in contrast to the switchback effect of the roadway to the left!

By 7 September 2008 all is laid in readiness and works trains and occasional specials have negotiated this new stretch. The roadway is still as it was, but the railway will not need much tweaking before it can accommodate the paying public from 2009. Whilst the proximity to the road will give tremendous views of the trains, it is to be hoped that car drivers will be aware of its narrowness and not leave their vehicles in dangerous positions! *Both MJS*

The route under the road bridge at Pitt's Head is yet another location that is very close to the surrounding water table and suffers from drainage problems. It was ever thus in the days of the original WHR and into the 1950s, when volunteers, attempting to lift redundant rail from the site, worked in extremely damp conditions, leading to the area becoming affectionately known as 'Garraway's Bath', after the General Manager of the FR at the time, who was overseeing matters. This view on 17 January 2005, looking south, amplifies the conditions facing the new railway's contractors. The bridge abutments were for a proposed cattle crossing that was never built.

Eighteen months later, on 8 September 2006, the railway has made great strides onwards but the inherent problem remains, as shown by the water-filled drainage channel installed to the left of the track. As explained on page 87 of Volume 2, the site derives its name from a huge rock, standing just to the right of this view, whose profile when viewed from the road from Rhyd Ddu bears an uncanny resemblance to Hogarth's cartoon of William Pitt the Younger, twice Prime Minister between 1783 and 1806. This pairing of images shows just some of the work necessary to prepare the railway for re-opening. *Both MJS*

Above The two alignments that once passed through the Beddgelert Forest twisted and turned in an attempt to reduce the gradient, as the railway dropped some 500 feet from Pitt's Head. On the final approach to Beddgelert station the later of the two routes took a slightly more circuitous route before crossing the access lane to Cwm Cloch. This is seen in 1996, looking towards the station site, with an A-frame stile taking walkers over fencing and the tree growth of the previous 70 years providing a near-tunnel effect. *Ron Hurst*

Below Seen on the same day, the bridge that once spanned the river close to Beddgelert station has disappeared, leaving the gaping hole for the unwary! Again looking south, the station site is in the centre distance, with the village espied in the valley below to the left. The trackbed has disintegrated slightly to the left on this side of the gap, further evidence of the problems faced by the new railway when re-entering Beddgelert. *Ron Hurst*

Pursuing a decidedly less than straight course through the Beddgelert Forest, with the railway mileage at 4½ compared to 3½ miles by road, the railway drops around 500 feet from the summit of 640 feet above sea level at Pont Cae'r Gors, shortly after passing Pitt's Head, and eventually finds its way into Beddgelert station. A little over 16 miles from Caernarfon, the first picture is close to a driver's-eye view of the approach from the north. In the undated view, probably from the late 1930s, the water tower stands sentinel in the centre, with the lamp room to the right and the station building to the left, closer to the village.

A similar view was captured during a visit in July 1988, when the tracks had been absent for around half a century and the sheep had become used to their casual strolls around the site. However, the railway is not dead, but merely sleepeth!

Very nearly twenty years later the railway has regained possession of the site and on 27 January 2008 the layout and formation of station and trackbed are plain to see. The water tower base still stands defiantly and there are plans for a replacement tank to be placed on top once more. With the new island platform on the far – village – side, the rails on this side have been restored over the old inspection pit. *WHR collection/Terry Gough, MJS collection/MJS*

With trains from both Caernarfon and Portmadoc terminating at Beddgelert, it became known as a frontier town, with passengers making a through journey having to change there. This was never a desirable state of affairs as, having found a seat at the start of their journey, they did not want to have to give it up part way through, but whether this had a major effect on traffic numbers is debatable. Such an operation is seen in the early 1930s; on the left Willie Hugh Williams stands by *Russell* as it waits to return north, having run round its train and re-coupled. To the right, Baldwin No 590 has arrived from Portmadoc and awaits the road to run round its stock and return south to the port. On what is obviously a summer day, there seems to be a reasonable number of travellers – sadly not a regular state of affairs.

The same view 70 years later shows the scene as it had been for most of that time, but about to be disturbed! On 8 September 2006 all is peace and quiet before the major transformation that was about to befall the site.

Less than two years later the vista is transformed. The winter aspect of 27 January 2008 allows the bare trees to permit wider views of the predominantly white houses in the village, and the mountain beyond looks more rugged in the winter light, but the greatest change has come about with the rapid transformation of the site and the arrival of the island platform, rails, works wagons, lights and flower beds. *WHR collection/MJS (2)*

Oh dear, what can the matter be? Two heads are better than one, but what impact will six have? A delightful variety of headgear is on view as much discussion and close attention is given to *Russell* as it stands next to the water tower at Beddgelert some time in 1935. The front end is jacked up and the half-oil-drum sander has been moved from its position on the middle of the buffer beam. The spare coupling hook hangs from the loco's water tank and a carriage stands on the pit road on the left, but whether this is from *Russell*'s train or not is unknown. It would be interesting to learn of the nature of the problem. *J. E. Simpson, NRM*

Moving to the right-hand edge of the shelf carrying the railway, we are again looking north and obtain a clear view of the goods shed and its position next to the main running line arriving at the station. Seen in July 1934, we also have a slightly fuller view of the lamp room on the left, with the ubiquitous water tower in front.

In the second view we are again present on a warm 8 September 2006 and see the very casual preparatory work being undertaken with a theodolite. The restricted width of land available to the railway at this location is even more apparent from this angle, with a steep drop on the right.

What a transformation! Not only has there been vision on the drawing-board, but also on the ground, where the contractors have eked every inch of space to provide a wide island platform around which the rails curve gracefully. The removal of bushes in the middle distance has allowed a platform length that can accommodate some 10-11 coaches. Note the new version of the water tower at the far end, and the pit road on the left, again with rails in place. The flowerbeds now await green fingers, and the lamp standards their light fittings. *F. M. Gates, WHR collection/MJS (2)*

On an unidentified day in 1935 *Russell* pauses at Beddgelert between duties after arrival of a train from Portmadoc. Mr Marks, the 'Station Master', oversees the uncoupling routine before the loco pulls forward and runs round its train ready for the return journey. Note the black numbers on the buffer beam, so painted by the FR when that railway took over the lease of the WHR in the previous year. The three-coach train – comprising the Gladstone coach, an ex-buffet car and a Pickering brake – was common at this time, as the number of passengers was generally not that great!
C. R. L. Coles, WHR collection

Above Between leaving the WHR and returning to North Wales, *Russell* was something of an itinerant locomotive! Initially employed on opencast iron-ore workings at Hook Norton in Oxfordshire, after overhaul in 1942 it subsequently decamped to Fayles Tramway in Dorset, where the track gauge was altered to 1ft 11½in to accommodate it! In this 1955 view it is the centre of attraction among the enthusiasts who are on a visit to the site, no doubt attracted by the loco's presence. *Roger Holmes, MJS collection*

Below Just weeks after the above view, *Russell* was rescued from Fayles and moved back to Wales, initially to the Talyllyn Railway, where it spent some years; this view, at Tywyn Wharf, is dated 25 June 1958. Without nameplate, it rests on a specially provided length of track. *Barry Hilton, MJS collection*

In a further view of the 'crossing point' at Beddgelert in full use, No 590 has run up from Portmadoc and run round its train ready to return south, while *Russell* has just arrived from the north, to connect. Judging by the macs and overcoats, the weather is none too warm, although it does not appear to be actually raining, as the travellers patiently wait for their respective trains to leave. The standard of around an hour between arrival at and departure from Beddgelert certainly did nothing to engender custom!

On 8 September 2006 there is peace and tranquillity once more, and a distinct lack of any evidence that this was once the site of a railway at all, let alone a station and journey changeover point! *F. C. LeManquais, WHR Heritage Group collection/MJS*

A variation in motive power and operations is seen in this view from 1935. *Moel Tryfan* has arrived at Beddgelert from Portmadoc, has run round its train and now awaits the arrival of the train from Dinas before returning south. A young family are in conversation with what appears to be Mr Marks, the 'Station Master', here in shirtsleeves. The low angle of the photograph shows the tidy nature of the station and provides a pleasing portrait.

More than 70 years later the view on 27 May 2007 shows work in progress in transforming the rural idyll into a working station once more. Theodolites are in use again, ensuring that the laying of tracks and the placing of the platform is in accordance with the plans. The right-hand 'down' line is now in place, along the edge of the shelf, with the rest of the site being given the necessary attention to create the new station. The base of the old water tower is seen just left of centre. *J. E. Simpson, WHR Heritage Group collection/MJS*

The southern exit from Beddgelert is through Goat Cutting and the Goat Tunnel, both so named after the nearby Goat Hotel. The entrance to the tunnel can just be discerned in the distance, beyond the footbridge over the track. This view from August 1934 includes the coal siding on the left, with its catch point protecting the main line. Note also the very tall telegraph pole and, just beyond the footbridge, the aqueduct that took water to the hotel from a reservoir higher up the hill to the right.

By 27 January 2008 the same view has seen many changes, not least in the very recent past. The southern end of the island platform can be seen, and the footbridge has disappeared, new building has appeared on the left-hand embankment, there is no longer any siding at this end, and the trees on the right have established a permanent foothold. *F. C. LeMarquais, WHR Heritage Group collection/MJS*

Climbing part way up the embankment at the entrance to the cutting and looking back to the station, this was the layout at Beddgelert in 1924, with, in addition to the station buildings already seen, the bookstall on the right; this was not to last too long after this portrait, as it blew down in October 1927! The coal siding snakes to the bottom right-hand corner of the picture.

More than 80 years later, on 25 May 2007, track has reappeared at the site, but while the down line mirrors the curve of the original, this new one is further over towards the village and more closely covers the site of the old station building. Virtually complete, the area of stone to the right will accommodate the base for the present-day version, with the possibility of refreshments again being sold here. Note the forward thinking on the left with the introduction of more drainage channels! *K. F. Antia, WHR Heritage Group collection/MJS*

BEDDGELERT TO PORTHMADOG

The Goat Tunnel was excavated through the hillside that faced the Portmadoc, Beddgelert & South Snowdon Railway when it was attempting to create its route south from Beddgelert. In this view from around 1905, looking north through the tunnel towards Beddgelert, three officials of the railway, with G. C. Aitchison on the right, pay

a visit to view progress. The track runs straight from the tunnel and prepares to cross the newly constructed bridge over the road into the village, but this route was abandoned by the WHR in 1922, the new line swinging to the bottom left-hand corner of this shot.

That deviation necessitated the removal of more rock from the left-hand hillside and the final route can be seen recreated here on 27 January 2008. Despite the passage of nearly 100 years and nature's attempts to reclaim her own, the tunnel portal and surrounding area are remarkably little changed. Note, again, the provision of the drainage channel to pre-empt future problems on the rebuilt railway. *Studio Eryri, WHR collection/MJS*

Right and below This view of the abandoned bridge over the A498 Beddgelert-Porthmadog road is dated 26 June 1956. Unattended apart from an occasional inspection to ensure safety for road traffic, it is incredibly free of undergrowth, with the parapets clearly visible. The road can just be seen in the lower right-hand corner.

Half a century has passed and still the view, on 27 May 2005, is very little altered, with just a few inches added to the girth of the surrounding trees. *H. C. Casserley, MJS collection/MJS*

Below Had the railway continued on its original course it would have crossed the valley on an embankment, with a bridge over an access point midway to the river. The supports for this bridge were actually constructed and still stand, isolated, in the middle of the field! This is the view from the truncated road bridge, showing the abandoned structures, on 26 June 1956. *H. C. Casserley, MJS collection*

Here we have a delightful portrait of the A498 road bridge when new. Probably around 1906, three ladies in their finery have walked from the village – just round the bend in the distance – to have their picture taken, together with a small girl who appears to be carrying three buckets. Perhaps she is collecting some of the animal fertiliser that appears to be liberally coating the road's rough surface! *NRM*

We are now on the 'new' route, the one followed after the abandonment of the PB&SSR's first thoughts. Leaving Beddgelert behind, we have passed the Cemetery crossing and are heading towards Bryn y Felin bridge. As seen on 26 June 1956, the trackbed has been abandoned following the ripping up of the tracks during the Second World War, with the culvert exposed and providing a trap for the unwary walker! Sheep safely graze on the hillside.

To provide a slightly more interesting present-day view and to place the trackbed within its geographical context at this point, the lens has been widened to incorporate the A498, running alongside then over the railway. The date is 27 January 2008 and the track gangs have made impressive progress south; the railway looks in fine shape ready to accommodate the hoards that will hopefully descend in 2009 and beyond, to enjoy the views and experience after the railway opens. Sheep still safely graze, but now separated from the rails by appropriate fencing. *H. C. Casserley, MJS collection/MJS*

Immediately before the railway crosses the Afon Glaslyn over Bryn y Felin bridge, the A498 road swings hard right to cross it, on its way towards Porthmadog. Made of concrete, it has withstood the ever-increasing volume and weight of traffic over the years, but, it has to be said, it is not exactly a thing of great beauty! In 1932 the camera looks back towards Beddgelert, showing how the railway is forced to twist its way through the opening.

The comparative view from 8 September 2006 shows the preparations to make the trackbed ready for ballast and rails. The acute angle between railway and road is again emphasised and the vertical metal supports are more clearly seen in this portrait. Trees are also more in evidence than before. Nothing lasts for ever, however, and the highways authority decreed that the bridge should be rebuilt, leading to the already laid track being temporarily covered in April 2008 while demolition of the roadway was under way. A new road was created to bypass the bridge temporarily, crossing the railway on the level on the far side of the bridge in this view. *D. Rendall, WHR collection/MJS*

Here is Bryn y Felin bridge in all its glory – well, not quite, as there are no rails over it. At Easter 1952 the Afon Glaslyn ripples peacefully underneath the bare structure, benign in comparison to its sometimes gibbous state after heavy rains. Again, not particularly beautiful but eminently functional, it had not survived the weather over the years sufficiently well to take the new railway and its potentially much heavier loads.

Forty-four years later the deteriorating condition is seen from the presence of a narrow footway across the bridge, with gates at both ends to protect walkers. Note how, in this sylvan setting from 1996, the bridge is high and dry above the river – again in benign state – and that trees are staking their claim to the trackbed.

Taken out of use in the early years of this century, the FR had still perforce to allow walkers to cross the waters, so, in conjunction with Snowdonia National Park and Gwynedd County Council, it constructed a wooden footbridge immediately to the Beddgelert side of the railway bridge on a completely new embankment. This stood in glorious isolation until a replacement, replica railway bridge could be provided. Back in its original place, utilising duly strengthened original piers, this is the view on 8 September 2006, with the trackbed in course of preparation for rails to once again be laid across the span. *David Morgan, MJS collection/Ron Hurst/ MJS*

Crossing the bridge and climbing a little gives this view of an unidentified England engine approaching the river crossing on its way to Beddgelert from Portmadoc, probably in 1925. The wide sweep of the river is mirrored by both the railway and the 'fisherman's' footpath between the two. The 1796-feet Moel-Ddu mountain looms in the distance.

The same view on 8 September 2006 shows the path that has been enjoyed by countless thousands over the previous 70 years, despite it never being an official footpath. An easy gradient, but not particularly smooth, the path does its best to hold back the prolific verdant growth.

It's amazing the difference a season makes! Now in winter, on 27 January 2008, the trees are bare and the whole ambience is changed, apart from the dramatic transformation on the ground. Tracks are once more in the Aberglaslyn Pass, tamped and ballasted, ready for the start of operations. The sinuous sweeps of the railway as it curves in tune with the river and climbs above the waters will give travellers magnificent views that are a tourist's dream and can in no way be rivalled from the road on the other side of the river. *WHR collection/MJS (2)*

The A498 road is seen once again to the left in this vista, with the Glaslyn cascading over large boulders below the railway. Seen in 1939, the track hugs the cliff side, complete with a retaining wall to restrain rock fall, as it leaves the 'long tunnel' and heads for a shorter one on its way up to Beddgelert. Even a cursory examination of the surrounding terrain causes one to admire the tremendous achievement of the navvies in creating this railway landscape, with little more than gunpowder and bare hands!

In an era of 'belt and braces', the rebuilding of the railway here was delayed until the right-hand retaining wall had been heightened to prevent a rock fall onto a train. The mere fact that the public had been walking here for years with no added protection from the authorities – not even fencing between the path and the slide down to the river – seems to have been conveniently overlooked! Rails are now back in their rightful place on 27 January 2008, fencing has been provided and the Glaslyn continues to rush down the valley. *A. E. Rimmer, WHR collection/MJS*

The southernmost 'long tunnel' may 'only' be 300 yards long, but the magnitude of the task of boring through the rocks can be judged from this view, from around 1905/6. Railway officials are again on their inspection tour. There had been plans for an Aberglaslyn Halt at this point, presumably on the left-hand side of this view, but this was never to come to fruition. Judging from the area today, the scheme does not seem to have been particularly feasible.

This area has alternated from no railway, to railway, to none again, and to the tracks being relaid once more. The scene on 26 January 2008 demonstrates yet another attraction of this line, the delightful arboreal surroundings and the promise of the 'ghost train' ride through the tunnel! Notice how nature has conspired to disguise the tunnel mouth from construction days. *Studio Eryri, WHR collection/MJS*

A wider view of the area around the tunnel does nothing to reduce the amazement at the navvies' achievements. In the early days after construction, judging by the apparent newness of the railway embankment, the switchback nature of the route is exemplified by the dramatic switch from mountain and tunnel to embankment. Cwm Bychan lies to the right, with, today, in the left foreground, a car park to entice walkers to enjoy the environment. The sight of the magnificent Garratt locomotives threading their way through this pass will no doubt encourage many to use the parking facility to good advantage. *WHR collection*

Having run from tunnel to open embankment on its journey south, the railway then immediately ran into cuttings on the either side of Nantmor! The second of the two was close to the bridge over the A4085 Llanfrothen-Beddgelert road. In this view, looking back towards the tunnels on 6 April 1977, tracks have been absent for more than 30 years and nature is doing her best to reclaim ownership.

Some of the overhanging trees have been removed during the restoration for safety reasons but, otherwise, the aspect is little changed on 26 January 2008, apart from the reappearance of rails. The railway has regained its straight line here, with the sharp bend at the far end approaching the site of the erstwhile Nantmor Halt. *Ray Ruffell, Silver Link Publishing collection/MJS*

Immediately over the road bridge mentioned opposite the line descends to the valley floor and leaves the rocks and towering heights well behind. Four miles further on the line again crosses the Afon Glaslyn, at Pont Croesor. Looking towards the ultimate goal in Porthmadog, the view on 16 September 1949 shows the B4410 Prenteg-Llanfrothen road alongside the railway, with the trackbed still in situ but without the rails.

On 3 November 2006 the supporting pillars are still in place on the riverbed but the original steelwork has been removed. New protective fencing has been placed between road and rail, tree growth has been healthy and the gorse in the foreground presents a 'Thou shalt not pass' stance!

Less than two years later, on 8 September 2008, the scene is very different. The railway has regained its passage over the river, the distant tree and attendant undergrowth have been removed and, though not fully appreciable in comparison with the earlier views, the river is now some feet above its normal level following heavy rains, and is now the full width of the bridge. At the far end of the bridge the entry to the Osprey Centre (on the left of the picture), previously off the elbow of the road as it curved over the railway, has been re-routed over a second level crossing some 50 yards to the south. *Ken Cope, Roger Carpenter collection/MJS (2)*

We are now on the northern outskirts of Porthmadog in the 1930s. Sadly the photograph has suffered a little with age, but it beautifully shows the transhipment area between the WHR and the Cambrian Railways, known as Beddgelert Sidings. The majority of the standard-gauge wagons on the right belong to the Pwllheli Granite Co, marshalled alongside a loaded narrow-gauge coal wagon that stands on the loop at the 1933 second Portmadoc 'New' station, which was more normally reserved for loco use when running round trains. Moel y Gest outcrop looms in the distance.

The view on 14 April 2008 is from the same vantage point, but the new rails have assumed a slightly different alignment. The line on the left is the resurrected narrow-gauge main line to Porthmadog, while the turnout towards the right takes us to Pen y Mount station and the entrance to the WHR site at Gelert's Farm. The station building, seen in the centre, has been modelled to faithfully recreate that which stood at Nantmor on the original railway. The footpath on the extreme left will give advantageous views of the trains when services are resumed after 70 years! *MJS collection/MJS*

Looking back towards the route we have travelled, Pen y Mount station is seen before the Nantmor-style waiting shelter was installed. In July 1988 the platform is bare apart from a rudimentary surface but, even on a dull summer's day, the appeal of seeing and riding behind *Russell* has not lost its pull!

How things have changed, not just on the ground but also in our society. Health & Safety considerations mean that the redeveloped WHR is now hemmed in with fencing on either side to 'protect the public', and the station platform is likewise segregated, in case any unsuspecting humans should inadvertently fail to notice a big steaming locomotive bearing down on them! Note the accurate replication of the Nantmor edifice, on 14 April 2008, even down to the correct corrugated iron structure. *Terry Gough, MJS collection/MJS*

Above Earlier in the same day as the upper picture on the previous page, *Russell* is captured at the front end of the train, indulging in a little shunting before setting back into the terminus station close to what was then British Rail's station in Porthmadog. To the left the railway's goods shed can just be glimpsed, alongside which was a platform for passengers to alight and tour the sheds, yard and sidings. *Terry Gough, MJS collection*

Below Even earlier in the day, *Russell* has yet to leave the yard and begin the day's duties. The railway's 1952-vintage Ruston & Hornsby diesel *Glaslyn* stands before the venerable steam loco, ready to give whatever assistance may be required. The aforementioned goods shed is seen more clearly on the right, while the engine shed looms behind the locos. Note the waste material in the wagons, ready to be carted away. *Terry Gough, MJS collection*

On the approach to the flat crossing with the ex-Cambrian Railways line, looking back once more, the exchange sidings can again be seen, with the loco loop recorded on page 60, now disconnected at this end, beyond the bare telegraph pole. Again, although the photograph has seen better days, it does show the layout when standard and narrow gauge operated cheek by jowl. The date is December 1924 and the first Welsh Highland Railway is in its first flush of youth!

As has been seen on some earlier pages, the new railway has not always slavishly followed the original alignment and this is also the case here. There are good operational reasons for this, but it will not deter the eventual enjoyment after the opening. With the line from Gelert's Farm terminus to Pen y Mount on the left, this view goes some way to recreating the earlier one, though, again, there is not the laissez faire approach previously enjoyed – as seen on 14 April 2008 pedestrians wanting to reach Pen y Mount by foot are now strictly channelled!
Adrian Gray collection, FR Archives/MJS

As already mentioned, the terminus of the WHR – the erstwhile ''64 Company' – is close to the standard-gauge facility in Porthmadog. In the early days of this section of the WHR preservation movement, the proximity is well portrayed in a view from the nearby War Memorial atop its promontory, with a semi-dismantled Bagnall 4-4-0T on display by the entrance. Note the sizeable signal box on the main line and old-style level crossing gates. Note also the cars in the parking area but the lack of them in the road, and the early booking office-cum-shop.

Progress is never-ending and, as with any other organisation, the WHR Ltd hierarchy has adapted and adjusted to changing fashions and public demands. The car park is now wholly changed with, it has to be said, a more formal but attractive public face; beyond, the standard gauge has moved with the times, with signal box and conventional gates having been dispensed with. The buildings on the far side of the railways, however, are little changed, as seen on 2 November 2006. *Studio Eryri, WHR collection/MJS*

The crossing of the two railways on the level at the northern edge of the town was a vital link to Harbour station and the FR in the early days. This view, looking south towards Portmadoc, is from 1923 and shows the arrangement in its heyday, with gates effectively protecting both railways and, to the right, the WHR's signal box, which was 'manned' for much of its time by a woman! The water tower that serviced thirsty locomotives, seen beyond the gates, stood by the station delightfully known as 'Portmadoc New'. Note the sign, helpfully stating 'Beware of Trains'!

As if to emphasise that this is, indeed, the same vantage point, the base of the water tower stands defiantly against progress and the passage of time, destined to see once again the passage of trains from 2009. On 4 August 2008 sleepers have been laid on both sides of the reinstated crossing and within weeks rails will have been attached and further ballast laid. The site of the signal box is destined to have a replica of the original, to the detriment of the present fir tree! *WHR Heritage Group collection/MJS*

Moving across the Cambrian line, we now look north towards Beddgelert in 1932 with the signal box on the left and a second gate in place on the northern approach. Note the 'Raleigh Cycles' advertising sign in the field alongside the railway. There were four basic versions of this sign, two in English, one in Welsh and one in Gaelic! In addition, the cyclist was at a different position along the sign and two did not have the '12 Miles' milepost. While most such signage was distributed to areas of high population density and/or potential points of sale, such as tobacconists, newsagents and other specialists, these Raleigh displays were deliberately placed in the countryside where transport was thin on the ground, in an attempt to woo the public to two wheels!

Following the installation of the new flat crossing – reinstating the original that had been lifted in 1938 – a modern gate has been placed closer to the main line than the earlier one, as seen on 14 April 2008. The replacement signal box will be installed where the fir tree stands, not as close to the standard gauge as the original but close enough – and to the original design – to satisfy both heritage and practical needs. *W. D. Miller, MJS collection/MJS*

Prince runs into Portmadoc New station, tender-first from Beddgelert, eagerly watched by two summer-hatted travellers. The photograph is undated, but would appear to be from around 1923 when the FR became involved in the operations of the then new WHR, judged partly because of the use of that company's England engine but also due to the uniform with its prominent insignia worn by the guard as he hangs from the coach vestibule, preparing to leap down to attend to the prospective passengers. Note that another train waits on the adjacent line, next to the water tower that is just visible above *Prince*'s cab.

With the encroachment of the adjacent land and the screening of this by a tall wire mesh fence, an exact recreation is neither possible nor desirable. However, even with the more restricted vista and the fencing, it is barely conceivable that there could have been sufficient land to accommodate all that is seen above. On 31 October 2006 work is beginning on clearance for the installation of the flat crossing, with the JCB digging out nearly 70 years of undergrowth. Once more the water tower is the location point. *Gwynedd Archives, John Keylock collection/MJS*

We have now moved to the water tower and are looking back towards the photographer's standpoint on the previous page. The sign on the left of the loco reads just 'Portmadoc', but the site, opened in 1923, has always been referred to as 'Portmadoc New', to differentiate it from the older FR Harbour station and the nearby ex-Cambrian standard-gauge facility. *Moel Tryfan* slows as it pulls into the station with a train from Harbour to Beddgelert, complete with its own style of sand bucket on the buffer beam. Again the guard – and driver – look ahead, perhaps keeping an eye on the two boys on the right, one with a box under his arm. Snowdon Flour Mill is in the background, just above *Moel Tryfan's* boiler.

Again, the comparative view shows just how much of the railway's land has been lost to bordrage on the far side of the fence. On 2 November 2006 three representatives of the contractors involved with the installation of the flat crossing and future developments discuss the situation, with Snowdon Mill still dominant in the background. *WHR Heritage Group collection/MJS*

Snowdon Mill is seen again, but this time from below the trackbed. As well as the Mill and the water tower base, this portrait from July 1988 shows the station building for Portmadoc New to the right, unusually at a lower level than the railway. Abandoned after trains ceased to run through to Harbour station from 1933, it still looks in reasonable condition here, and would manage to survive for approaching another decade before finally collapsing in the late 1990s and being removed.

Were it not for the Mill, the water tower and the two buildings on the extreme right linking these two views, it would be hard to say that this was the same location! By 2 November 2006 yet more fencing in the foreground and midway across the old field has appeared, together with an inordinate amount of detritus in the space between it and the railway. Aping a periscope, the water tower defiantly proclaims the railway's position. *Terry Gough, MJS collection/MJS*

Moving slightly closer to the town and looking back towards the flat crossing – note the signal box in the distance, between coach and loco – the layout at Portmadoc New is again seen. In this photograph from the 1930s the station building can be seen at the lower level to the left of the coach, with a light-coloured roof at this date and without the front extension that was to grace it in later years. Double-Fairlie *Taliesin* has brought a short train from Harbour station, but trains are no longer crossing the Cambrian, forcing passengers wishing to travel further to cross the standard-gauge line by foot and join the WHR train on the far side adjacent to Beddgelert Sidings.

Road vehicles of various shapes and models proliferate on both sides of this 4 August 2008 view, but the railway is defiantly reclaiming its right of passage. Sleepers are laid on site and the rails are following, as members of the Rest of the World Gang indulge their passion for volunteering and furthering the rebuilding of the line. *Roger Kidner, WHR Heritage Group collection/MJS*

This final look at Portmadoc New is from a slightly elevated vantage point in around 1923. Another England engine has arrived at the station and there seems to have been quite a throng that have detrained and are making their way into town. Note that the station building is new and completely white, with steps up to the platform level. The long building in the background houses what looks to be a rather palatial Refreshment Room. A box van and loaded wagon wait on the second line. Also note the clear field to the right and the generally open nature of the whole scene. *Lens of Sutton Collection, MJS collection*

A second road crossing on the journey south from Beddgelert was adjacent to Snowdon Mill, but once trains stopped crossing the Cambrian line in 1933 there was little use for the stretch between Harbour and Portmadoc New other than movement of flour to Penrhyn via the FR. The Ffestiniog ceased operations in August 1946 and the track to Snowdon Mill was severed some time thereafter. This truncation can be seen in the foreground of this 16 September 1949 photograph, with the track still crossing the road, then curving to the right towards the site of Portmadoc New and left past the greenhouse to a slate mill, on a stub of the Gorseddau Tramway, closed in 1892. The three-storey Mill towers over its surroundings.

By 28 January 2008 preparations are well under way for the restoration of rails over the road, which would be achieved within six months. In the foreground the recent excavations to properly install the necessary drainage pipes have been completed and the gaping holes repaired. Elsewhere, the telegraph poles have been re-sited, but the Mill, the right-hand wall and the far hillside are little changed. *Ken Cope, Roger Carpenter collection/MJS*

We have now reached the town of Portmadoc on a bright and sunny 9 August 1935, to witness Baldwin No 590 leaving Britannia Bridge and swinging into Madoc Street on its way north to Beddgelert, with one of the brightly coloured Ashbury coaches in tow. Note that cycles outnumber cars!

Unlikely as it may seem, this is the view in the 21st century. The low building on the left is common to both scenes, but otherwise the transition to modern living is complete. By 26 January 2008 shops have largely taken over the erstwhile goods yard on the far side of the main road into town; the wall extension to the low building has been removed and the space now belongs to a filling station; and while there are plenty of motor vehicles there are definitely no cycles! *H. F. Wheeller, Roger Carpenter collection/MJS*

After taking the upper photograph on the previous page, the photographer has moved towards the main road and, turning round, captures No 590 passing the London-registered ALD 305 and slowly making its way along the street before negotiating the curve past the white house in the centre distance.

Much of the street ahead and the visible buildings have changed relatively little over the intervening 73 years, but at this end the junction with the main road has been redesigned to accommodate the exit from and entrance to the filling station. On 26 January 2008 the street on the far side of the 'Araf'/'Slow' sign on the roadway is now 'one way'. *H. F. Wheeller, Roger Carpenter collection/MJS*

The A497 road into Porthmadog has long been a scene of nose-to-tail motor traffic trying to negotiate its way through the town. In 1947, however, the picture is a very different one, with the country still recovering from the deprivations of war and before the explosion of car ownership. Following the rails out of Madoc Street, we look across Britannia Bridge towards Britannia Terrace on the left and the FR's Harbour station, beyond the building in the centre mid-distance. Note the Harbour branch disappearing into grass on the right, with the erstwhile goods yard now out of use, and the 'Portmadoc UDC' sign offering 'Free Parking'!

Again, there is much change and little change. Britannia Terrace and the FR's station have not moved, but otherwise progress has brought much alteration over the ensuing 60 years. On 26 January 2008 rails have still to make their appearance over the bridge, but preparations for this are ongoing to the left; the bridge parapet is higher, but the high wall on the right in the earlier view has gone, leading to a more open view of the water below, and a completely new residential development has sprung up on the far side of the bridge. *J. I. C. Boyd, John Keylock collection/MJS*

Turning round from the photographs on the previous page, we are now looking down High Street on 16 September 1949, with the railway crossing from Madoc Street and skirting the inside of the bridge parapet. In the foreground the two tracks that led to the goods yard and wharfs are out of use and are becoming silted up and overgrown. The large building in the centre is a motor garage, complete with pumps outside by the pavement, and on the extreme right are the Maenofferen Quarry offices.

  By 26 January 2008 all is change. The rails have gone – and will not be returning to their old route – as have the delightful trees around the garage; the bridge now has a pavement, running roughly where the tracks used to be; the road is a much more formal affair; and the Quarry offices have been in retail use for many years. Also noticeable are the number of street lights now in place and the greater number of cars visible. *Ken Cope, Roger Carpenter collection/MJS*

Above Don't try this at home! Some 15 or so years before the date of the 'past' view opposite we have a potential calamity. Quite often in today's press there are reports of motorists trying to dodge over level crossings in the path of a train, but it is obviously not a new phenomenon! In an undated view from around early 1933 *Taliesin* swings across the road – with a full complement, by the look of it – whistle sounding, as a driver dices with death! Note the tall, rather unusual telegraph pole on the left and the cars, which look as though they have just driven out of a Laurel and Hardy film! *WHR Heritage Group collection*

Below A year later, in 1934, what appears to be *Welsh Pony* is photographed from the train, travelling in the opposite direction and most definitely in less than desirable weather conditions! In pouring rain, a lady tries her best to keep at least part of herself dry under an umbrella. *Roger Kidner, WHR Heritage Group collection*

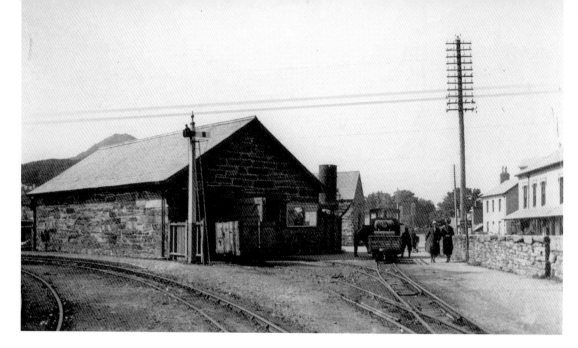

And so we arrive at the Ffestiniog Railway's Harbour station. Some time in the 1930s the Baldwin diesel-hauled freight pauses on the WHR tracks into the station while its cargo is inspected and two ladies casually saunter by. Britannia Terrace stands to the right, the FR tracks run into the platform on the left, and there are two sidings running into the substantial goods shed, with a water tank just beyond. Another of the distinctive telegraph pole 'trees' stands at the side of the A497 road, but seemingly without wires!

By 16 September 1949 – three years after the closure of the FR – the scene is rather different! Tracks are still in situ, with slate wagons where they were abandoned, the goods shed doors are firmly closed, the telegraph pole has just two horizontals remaining, and the water tank has disappeared. Nature is enjoying a free hand.

Following rescue by enthusiasts in 1954, the FR has done wonders to resurrect the site and make it a true tourist attraction. Part of this, however, saw the removal of the rails that once brought the WHR into the station, but, with the rebuilding of the WHR rapidly approaching its next milestone, thought has turned to once more providing a way in for the new railway. On 14 April 2008 a point has been inserted into the platform road, showing intent and the way forward. The old goods shed is now Spooner's Bar & Restaurant and, to the left, the building has seen infilling to provide café, shop and booking office facilities. *John Keylock collection/Ken Cope, Roger Carpenter collection/MJS*

Above To conclude this part of our journey, we take a look at WHR No 590 in Porthmadog. On 8 August 1935 the engine has brought its train from Beddgelert and indulges in a little shunting of coaching stock before returning north. The fireman is about to climb back aboard. *H. F. Wheeller, Roger Carpenter collection*

Below The following day No 590 has crossed the mile-long Cob embankment and has taken temporary refuge in Boston Lodge yard. Although coal and water were available at Harbour station, the reason for the Works visit could be to avoid smoke nuisance to residents of Britannia Terrace. *H. F. Wheeller, Roger Carpenter collection*

CONSTRUCTION VIEWS

In a departure from normal 'Past & Present' practice, and also from Volumes 1 and 2 of this series, you are now going to be treated to a selection of images that places the cynosure squarely on the construction of the railway. A largely unseen – and probably unthought of – area of the rebuilding, it is necessarily a vital ingredient that all the groundwork is done correctly before trains actually run. Many hundreds of people have been involved over the years, and I dedicate this section to them to thank them all for their part in the continuing story. All photographs are by the author unless otherwise credited.

Above No railway can function without tracks and these need something to keep them in place. Normally this is achieved by the strategic use of stone ballast, piled under and around the sleepers, and on 11 April 2004 a rake of appropriately loaded wagons awaits the call just north of Dinas station yard, behind the railway's Matisa tamper.

Left Here is the tamper five months later, on 11 September 2004, in use beside Dinas platform. For the uninitiated, tamping is a means of vibrating the stones around the sleepers to remove any unwanted air pockets and ensure that the track is settled on a firm and level surface. This is done by vibrating tines – spade-like paddles – on either side of the sleeper, on both sides of the tamper. Depending on the size of machine, there can be several tines on each side, but here there are just two, seen resting on the ballast just behind the cab door.

Above As anyone will know who has tried to lay sand level enough to take slabs, or who has attempted to level ground for a 'bowling green' lawn, creating that 'billiard table' effect can be frustratingly difficult! With the larger size and unevenness of ballast stones, preparing a railway trackbed is even harder, so it is to the credit of all concerned that it is possible to achieve the effect seen here at Dinas on 18 April 1998, just six months after the line opened to here from Caernarfon.

Below Construction does not, of course, stop with the groundwork – locomotives are also needed. On 29 August 1999 work is focussed on ex-South African NG15 No 134 outside Dinas engine shed. In pretty run-down shape when received by the new WHR, the restoration would of necessity be a long-term project, to be fitted in with available manpower and finance. Since this photograph was taken progress has been snail-like, but recently a fresh start has been made.

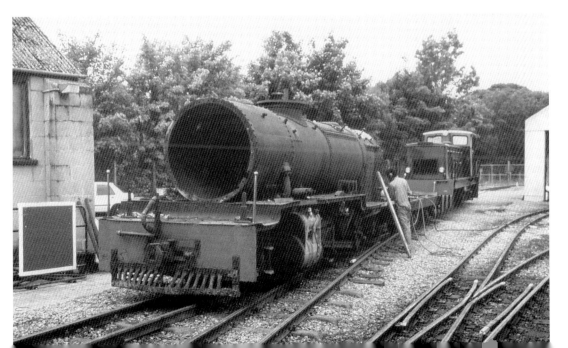

These two views show trackbed preparation at Cae Moel, just east of Dinas. As explained on page 25 of Volume 2, this bridge was originally a triple – road over railway and both over a river beneath. On the right at the far side of the bridge remedial action had to be taken to divert the river before the course of the railway could be fashioned. On this side access for machines was from the roadway, across the ground adjacent to the line's low embankment, and the results can be seen in this view from 5 February 2000. The trackbed has had an initial deposit of ballast and the roller is consolidating it.

By the following 14 July further attention has been given to the trackbed and rails have passed through Bridge 16. Note how the surrounding ground has also been 'improved'! The rails are not yet clipped into their chairs, hence the apparently disturbing gauge variation!

Above Another major consideration of the rebuilding was to repair and/or rebuild bridges and culverts that had fallen into disrepair during the 60-plus years that the trackbed had been abandoned. The opportunity was also taken to foster good relations with the railway's neighbours by, in many cases, improving the previous facilities and even, on occasion, incorporating some of the re-use of the alignment by, for example, farmers. Roughly midway between Tryfan Junction and Waunfawr, progress on the rebuilding and improvement of underbridge UB25 is captured on 5 February 2000.

Right In the distance in the view above can be seen a bridge across the track. On the same day this bridge, allowing a farmer access to his field and allocated code number OB24, is in the process of being rebuilt, with wooden shuttering in place for the sides and metal supports beneath. Note also the new fencing that the railway was having to provide. This was necessary, in varying styles, for much of the 26-mile route, and consequently became a major expenditure within the overall budget.

Above With periods of heavy rain over the winter of 1999/2000, the new railway had to contend not just with preparing and rebuilding the trackbed but also, on occasions, having to shore up collapsed infrastructure. Access to many of these out-of-the-way lineside locations was only via the trackbed, and one such location was on the approach to Waunfawr, when the very wet conditions led to landslips. On 5 February 2000 yet another load of stone to repair the hillside is transported over the route of the old railway.

Below Finally, the way was made safe and works trains could proceed to the new areas to consolidate the work, attend to upcoming problems or merely to transport men and tools. This journey up the line behind *Upnor Castle* took place on 14 July 2000. Note the new fencing on the right, and a farmer's access gateway.

The development of Waunfawr is seen earlier in this book, but another view of the early days of transformation is captured on 28 July 1999. Prayers that the weather would improve, being the height of the summer period, went unanswered, as is plainly evident here, with the railway entering the site under the road bridge on the extreme right on this dull day. The original station building still stands, awaiting the numbering of the stones and bricks and the dismantling that was to prove so otiose.

Once again a comparative view shows the scale of the achievements as the railway progressed. Seven years on from the above view, on 8 September 2006, the layout is now well established, looking for all the world as though this was how it had always been! Platform signs clearly announce the location and the recently introduced flowerbeds begin to make the place much more homely.

Above The curving nature of the track as it enters Waunfawr from Dinas can be judged from the lower picture on the previous page, and is clear again in this view from 14 July 2000. Complete with high-visibility apparel, a track gang responds to 'Once more!' and pulls together to gradually move the rails into the desired position on what will be the down road, towards Rhyd Ddu. Waunfawr platform will eventually end roughly in line with the gang in this shot. The next job will be the ballasting of the track, tamping and ensuring that all is duly in place for the first trains.

Below Moving forward just two months, the track gangs have left and it is a case of 'hold your nerve' as Garratt No 143 thunders into Waunfawr with the first public train on 15 September 2000. The gauge may only be 2 feet, compared with the 4ft 8½in standard gauge, but the locomotives are no toys! With Plaid Cymru MP Dafydd Wigley leaning out of the cab, thoroughly enjoying his time 'playing trains', two female members of the Stretton family hold the supports for the banner, desperately hoping it will break and not drag them under!

Above It might be imagined that replacing access points for the railway's neighbours would be straightforward, but in these days of Health & Safety this is most definitely not the case. On the long straight stretch south of Waunfawr, the complexity of the construction of what might appear to be a simple farm crossing can be judged from this view on 12 October 2001 – not just the actual crossing itself but protection at all four corners, not least to keep animals (and humans!) off the track.

Below As already seen at Cae Moel, the railway also crosses various streams and rivers. Immediately south of Betws Garmon station there was another tricky situation. Not only was the line to cross the Afon Gwyrfai, with the original bowspring bridge not adequate to take the increased weight of today's locos and trains, but also the many years of heavy rains had scoured the shallow embankments on both sides of the river, leading to new abutments being required. Once more these were to be more substantial than previously, and the new 'seats' for the metalwork are seen, newly in position, on 1 June 2003.

Hearts are in mouths as the new bridge is gingerly lowered into place on 5 June 2003! As explained in *Volume 2*, WHR Society members financed the replacement. Being too expensive to build from new, this involved sourcing a suitable second-hand item – eventually a redundant Network Rail bridge from near Rotherham – transporting it to the site and preparing it for placement. It had originally been a skew bridge and needed here to be square; there was precious little room for redesign but, happily, *just* enough! It went into place at the first attempt, with millimetres to spare, and has proved to be up to the job ever since. Further views of the crossing before and after appear in Volume 2.

Turning through 180 degrees, the way ahead is seen with work in progress on 1 June 2003. With the renowned Elephant Mountain in the background, the shallow embankment has been transformed from its previous unkempt look and smoothed from its switchback condition, having been left to nature for nearly 70 years. A ballast bed is in place and space has been retained at the site of the erstwhile Halt to incorporate a loop during the reconstruction process, together with a new station.

Further up river, the bowstring bridge at Plas y Nant proved to be sufficient for the new operation but a complication here was that the original had been used for many years after abandonment as access for a local landowner. Once more, the railway has been good-neighbourly, incorporating the innovation of placing a new access alongside the bridge, away from trains and tracks. This newer arrangement, together with the newly laid track – and catch rails – is seen on 8 September 2006.

Above Looking back towards the river bridge seen on the previous page, the temporary loop and new Halt are now in place and await their first travellers on 8 September 2006. The loop was subsequently dispensed with.

Below Another completely new station – the original site being unavailable – was at Snowdon Ranger, between Plas y Nant and Rhyd Ddu. With the original building in private occupation and no room to fit the station into the remaining corridor, the new site is a little to the south. When seen on 2 June 2003, with storm clouds gathering, the basic platform structure is in place, with fence posts erected. The dumper stands on what will be the trackbed, while consideration is given by the gentlemen along the platform as to what needs to be done next.

While the trackbed on the approaches to Rhyd Ddu was intact after 70 years, the route into and immediately past the old station was not, having been appropriated by the Snowdonia National Park as the roadway to a car park on the site, thus the new railway had yet another problem to surmount. The solution was to purchase a wedge-shaped strip of land on the Snowdon side of the original site and create a wholly new station. In the early days after purchase, on 12 October 2001, fencing has been installed, marking out the boundary within which the railway will operate. The old trajectory lies in front of the toilet block sandwiched between the two clumps of trees to the right.

A slightly wider view on 1 June 2003 sees the station built and acting as the temporary southern terminus, but not yet complete or open for traffic. The fencing and the toilet block are again seen, with *Conway Castle* and *Upnor Castle* in the platforms on works trains.

Somewhat resembling a caterpillar – or an N gauge model – Garratt No 143 is seen negotiating the Fridd Isaf curves on the final approach to Rhyd Dd 1 with its six coaches and cycle wagon on 10 April 2004. The village stands in readiness for the train that, arriving at lunchtime, may despatch some of its passengers to the public house seen upper left! The line has been open a mere nine months at this stage but is already proving its popularity with locals and tourists alike, in addition to the obvious appeal to the enthusiasts. The curvature of the route from Snowdon Ranger, with the flank of the mountain looming ever closer, provides this stretch of the new line with magnificent and breathtaking views, not least across to Quellyn Lake. Visitors should be aware, however, that much of the land seen here is private property, and this photograph was taken with permission.

At Rhyd Ddu the single track divides to provide a loop, with tracks on either side of the new island platform. On a dull 2 June 2003, with the old alignment to the right of the trees, *Conway Castle* shunts its works train into the up platform, closely watched by the day's track gang.

It is often overlooked that a railway is much more than trains, track and stations. We have already seen the provision of protective fencing, but in this view, on 26 January 2008, there is also a telegraph pole, lighting, delightful seating (courtesy of the WHR Society) and, of no little significance, a large water tower. Being something of an outpost – certainly in its time as a terminus – Rhyd Ddu needed facilities to quench the thirsts of hard-worked steam locomotives.

Mention of track leads us to a portrait of one of the specially constructed track components, into which has been cast 'WHLR 12', seen immediately to the south of Rhyd Ddu station on 21 January 2007.

No sooner had the railway settled into the routine of running trains to Rhyd Ddu, halfway along the full route, than thoughts turned in earnest to Phase 4. Nominally the easier half of the route, there were still problems ahead, not least yet more improved drainage requirements. As seen earlier in this volume, Pitt's Head is the location of long-standing trouble, and the view on 2 May 2005 – the May Day Bank Holiday! – shows most unseasonable conditions. The road into Rhyd Ddu is seen to the left, with the trackbed to the right, just inside the fencing, and a new channel dug between to take away the waters in the early stages of construction.

By 8 September 2008 the area has a wholly different look, with the drainage successfully channelled, much of it in concrete pipes, and the track laid. Though properly ballasted, tamped and ready for use, the stretch from Rhyd Ddu to Pitt's Head was 'fine-tuned' for alignment a month after this view. Note that a low retaining wall has been added to further protect the railway.

At Pont Cae'r Gors the railway reaches the summit of the line and enters the Beddgelert Forest, having run through open countryside from Pitt's Head. As can be seen in this view from that wet 2 May 2005, the preceding 70 years have witnessed prolific tree growth, necessitating a fair degree of logging to re-establish the trackbed. Looking back towards Rhyd Ddu, evidence of this lies in the foreground, as a tracked excavator approaches from the open stretch to carve out the railway's route once more.

Hardly recognisable as the same location, the way has been cleared and prepared and the track laid by 8 September 2006. Subsequent work would see works trains running to and beyond this point by the end of the year. Comparing these two photographs shows just how much had to be contended with in restoring a line that had succumbed to other influences over the preceding seven decades.

Left We are now in the Forest and approaching the first of the two large 'double-horseshoe' S-bends that take the railway down a rapidly falling gradient. For those fortunate (or intrepid!) enough to have walked this route prior to improvements, yet more boggy conditions made the task almost impossible at times. Thus yet more major work was involved to create an effective trackbed, and some of the groundwork is seen here on 14 October 2006, entailing yet more drainage culverts alongside the track within freshly excavated lapidose cuttings. A works train gingerly negotiates the beginning of the sharp curve, delivering more rail to the 'head of steel', just yards ahead of it.

Below left Three months and half a mile or so further on, by 21 January 2007 the 'head of steel' has passed the site of the new station for the Forest Campsite and reached Tyn-y-Coed. While some of the sharper curves have had the rails pre-formed, the rest is a case of bending to shape. Here one rail is fixed in the chairs on the sleepers, but the right-hand one still awaits its turn for coaxing into position.

Above I make no excuses for including this picture of a motley crew with cheesy grins! Unlike standard-gauge lines, where machines do much of the 'heavy' work, narrow gauge is in constant and sometimes desperate need of volunteers who are not afraid to get their hands dirty. Again seen at Tyn-y-Coed on 21 January 2007, the gang take a short breather to have their portrait taken – and they are not exclusively male, with a 'gun-toting' lady much more than a nominal member of 'the fairer sex'! Like all their colleagues elsewhere on the railway, the 11 individuals here – one for the first time – deserve the greatest degree of praise and gratitude from the rest of us 'armchair' supporters, for without them we would not have a railway to enjoy. Hopefully, their happy faces will encourage new volunteers to join them.

Beddgelert was a 'frontier town' on the original WHR, being the destination of trains from both Porthmadog and Dinas, with passengers generally having to change here; it is to be hoped that travellers are not asked to similarly change their seats on the new railway. Rebuilding from the original layout at this location saw much head-scratching as, like Waunfawr and Rhyd Ddu, it was to be an island platform, and the first track beside it is seen roughly laid in position on 25 May 2007. Due to the width of the platform and the current thinking regarding clearances, this line is running close to the edge of the shelf on which the old station stood.

The view on 27 January 2008 is impressive. The platform is fully laid, with lamp standards in place, a flowerbed ready for plants and tracks on both sides, together with the relaid siding over the pit behind the base of the old water tower. Prevented from being a temporary terminus by the National Park Authority as building continued towards Porthmadog, it will, nevertheless, not have long to wait from this view and will surely be a real addition to the already tourist 'honeypot' that is Beddgelert.

Moving to the southern end of the station site on 25 May 2007, the curvature of the railway into the Goat cutting beyond is plain to see. The base of the old station building is subsumed beneath this new development and a contemporary building will be provided to the left of the Portaloo! Note yet more concrete drainage channelling on the right.

By 27 January 2008 yet more progress is obvious. Looking from the embankment beneath the white house in the above view, the station layout can be seen, together with the base for the new station building, which will provide modest refreshment facilities as well as a waiting room and ticket office. The sharp drop towards the village on the right is also clear in this shot. Wagons from a works train stand in the platform.

The entrance to the Goat cutting has long been a boggy place, only accessible to the intrepid or foolhardy. On 8 September 2006, it is yet another view of a railway that temporarily sleepeth!

What a difference nine months makes. Much hard work and planning has most definitely gone into this next step south, with not just the clearance of previous undergrowth but yet more concrete drainage and some further attention to the embankment stonework. Note the turnout under the footbridge, to bring the rails into the other side of the platform.

On the approach to Bryn y Felin bridge, the railway curves behind a house and briefly runs on the level beside the Beddgelert-Porthmadog road. Looking back towards Beddgelert on 17 October 2005 the road is to the right and the house is just visible between the two trees directly beyond the car. The trackbed disappears under the growth of the 'twilight years', passing the car to the left and running straight ahead. This short stretch has long been a handy pull-in, not least to enjoy the view to Beddgelert across the meadows.

The pull-in disappeared with the reappearance of the railway, as can be seen in the view from 27 January 2008. The railway has been slightly raised with the relaying of track, protective fencing has been installed and all is ballasted in preparation for the trains.

All was not straightforward, however, as the highways authority decreed that the road bridge over the railway adjacent to Bryn y Felin river bridge needed to be replaced. This entailed building a completely new roadway while the road bridge was removed and a new one built, and the result can be seen here on 16 April 2008, with track embedded in tarmac and the railway's fencing removed. Traffic would very soon be crossing the tarmac in the foreground, but only as a temporary measure, as the new bridge was in place for the re-opening of the railway in 2009!

Frustratingly, the removal of the bridge proved not to be a simple affair. Not least was the sheer strength of the concrete of the supporting walls and the National Park's requirement for the bridge to be rebuilt as close as possible to the original. It has never been a thing of great beauty and many felt that a new stone-faced structure would be more in keeping with the locality, but it was not to be. However, the methods of mixing the precise style of concrete are not standard today and this dictated further complications. In addition, protection had to be given to the rails already laid beneath, as a tracked excavator needed to access the route during demolition; a membrane was therefore placed over the track. Two diggers and a dumper truck are seen at work on 29 April 2008.

In advance of the road bridge replacement, that carrying the old trackbed over the Afon Glaslyn needed urgent attention, as it was in no state to carry the new railway. Its removal was sadly mourned by enthusiasts, but it also created a side issue: the need to retain a foot crossing over the river at this point meant the installation of a wholly new footbridge. A new rail bridge, faithful to the old design, was eventually put in place and is seen here, with the footbridge alongside, on 25 May 2007. The old road bridge can be seen beyond.

By 27 January 2008 the rails are back and walkers are discouraged from trespassing on the structure by the fencing leading from the footbridge.

More than 60 years of human feet tramping along the Aberglaslyn Pass over the former trackbed not surprisingly wreaked some havoc on the foundations, leading to more major work than might have been anticipated. Some of this is under way on 25 May 2007, on the southern approach to Bryn y Felin. The footbridge over the river can just be seen on the left, with notices warning present-day walkers to 'Give way to construction traffic' and to the contractors to 'Be aware of pedestrians'. The riverside pathway is now closer to the water and at the lower level.

The signs are still there on 27 January 2008, but elsewhere the work is complete, the formation has been duly repaired and shaped and the track is back in place, quite probably in much better shape than when the earlier line was laid! The start of the Fisherman's Path is seen to the left.

Further along the 'lonesome trail', on 25 May 2007, the contractor's markers are in place along the trackbed, but it is still looking very much as it had for the past six decades, with the exception of a small amount of preparatory stone placed on the formation. The Fisherman's Path has also seen some remedial action, with fresh stones placed at strategic points to ease passage alongside the river. With trees in new leaf, the scene is one that will readily be appreciated by travellers when the trains eventually return.

Looking for all the world like a Welsh version of a road through the Rockies, the tracks are back on 27 January 2008, with fresh fencing on both sides of the railway. The Glaslyn looks decidedly peaceful through the winter trees, as we face towards the Snowdon mountain range in the distance.

Another bridge that needed to be replaced was that crossing the A4085 Beddgelert-Llanfrothen road, south of the Pass and its tunnels. The view on 8 September 2006 shows the situation after the removal of the original span; happily, the two supporting parapets were of sufficient strength and were left to support the new bridge.

Less than two months later, on 30 October, the newly designed bridge has been very recently installed and work is beginning to make it safe and functional. The space for the rails has been prepared, and pedestrian access for railway staff on either side is also being installed. Looking ahead towards Porthmadog, the trackbed runs straight, on a swift down gradient to the valley floor and what may one day be Hafod y Llyn Halt.

By 26 January 2008 track has been installed and ballasted and the short straight stretch is clear to see. Hafod y Llyn will be located just a little further on past the curve of the track in the distance, beyond the tree 'tunnel'.

Above The previously mentioned straight stretch of track is in the centre of this panoramic view from 21 March 2008; the test train seen on page 6 has passed through the Aberglaslyn tunnels and is crossing the Nantmor bridge and running down the gradient to the valley floor. From this distance, No 143 again looks more like a model than a full-sized loco with perhaps only the white smoke indicating reality. Note the hairpin bend in the road just ahead of the train, the severity of which has taken more than one driver by surprise! *Alasdair Stewart*

Left Although approached by a very narrow, rocky and twisting lane, the site of the proposed Hafod y Llyn Halt is spacious. Continual replenishment of both men and machines is vital as work progresses and, as the railway proceeds south from Aberglaslyn, the area is here being used as a store for locomotive, stock and materials. On 14 April 2008 a digger and the remains of a works train are stationed between duties, with the running line visible to the left. In the bright early spring sunshine, the Snowdon mountain range is unusually clear.

The next major obstacle to be faced on the push south was Pont Croesor. Built to replace nearby earlier crossings of the Glaslyn, the road, now the B4410 from Llanfrothen to Prenteg, turned through 90 degrees immediately at the end of the existing rail bridge, constructed years previously by the Croesor Tramway and inherited by the original WHR. This view from 25 May 2007, with the Glaslyn in a benign mood, shows the roadway on the right and the stone piers of the former railway still in position after 70 years of disuse.

The original piers were built upon and augmented to recreate the railway crossing, and in this view from 26 January 2008 the basic construction is in place but as yet without track. With the road running immediately behind the photographer, the sharpness of its turn can be judged. At this point the access to the RSPB's Osprey Centre was still from the far elbow of the 90 degrees bend (out of sight on the right of this shot), but would subsequently be altered once rails had been laid over the road.

Seen again on 25 May 2007, the road layout that had served for more than half a century is plain to see. Standing on what had been the trackbed, the railway is masked by tarmac, the protective barrier and tree growth, as we look towards the majestic Cnicht mountain in the distance. The entrance to the Osprey Centre is in the right foreground.

By 14 April 2008 Cnicht is still visible in the background and the road's protective barrier is still in situ, but the bridge has reappeared and now has track on its deck. The Glaslyn still looks benign, but is higher than previously following recent rainfall.

The date of the third view is 5 August 2008 but, despite being nominally summer, the mist is low over the mountains and down to the fields in the middle distance, and your photographer is standing in horizontal drizzle! The bend in the road is as before, but rails now cross the tarmac and the entrance to the Osprey Centre is behind the camera. *Upnor Castle* stands at the far end of the bridge – the furthest point for a loco to reach at this date – with men at work on the track, and traffic lights control passage over the road bridge, at the far end and out of sight to the left at this end. Note the facility for foot crossing by staff over the rail bridge, as at Nantmor. On this day the Glaslyn was even higher, filling the whole width of the rail bridge and, off camera to the right, lapping at the ground by the Osprey Centre.

Standing on the end of the rail bridge and looking towards Porthmadog, this was the sight on 26 January 2008. The trackbed is discernible, but there is still much to be done to return this stretch to railway use. Evidence of work recently undertaken is by the uprooted tree stump and the Portaloo!

In the horizontal drizzle on 5 August 2008, a little over six months later, the railway has made a great leap forward, with track now over the road and over a second level crossing at the entrance to the Osprey Centre. Beyond, the smooth trackbed is laid out and ready for rails and for further ballast to be deposited. Land is being prepared for a loop line to be laid and a possible Halt for trains to deposit visitors to the Centre.

On the northern approach to Porthmadog, the old trackbed approaches the long-time home of WHR Ltd (previously known as the '64 Company) at Gelert's Farm. On 29 April 2005, with that railway's terminus at Pen y Mount behind the camera, work is in hand to turn the previous trackbed-cum-footpath into a railway once more. Formation work and initial ballasting have taken place and track is imminent, to once again provide access to the town from the north by rail. Cnicht can again be seen in the left distance.

With track-laying being undertaken from Pen y Mount northwards, to eventually meet the gangs moving south, this was the view at the southern 'head of steel', at Traeth Mawr, on 2 November 2006. Once more Cnicht is determined to dominate the skyline, overlooking the temporary loop that will be replaced when the line is joined up and a run-round facility is no longer needed. Note the uneven rail surface prior to tamping.

Above When track is first laid and ballasted it requires tamping to ensure as smooth a ride as possible before public trains can traverse it. Before this happens even works trains have to be careful and, although distorted by the effect of a telephoto lens, the crew of the two locos about to gingerly pass over the new track at Pen y Mount will need to have their wits about them to prevent accidents! The station building stands to the left of the track on 5 May 2008, while to the right a couple of bystanders watch the proceedings with interest. *Cliff Thomas*

Below A little nearer Porthmadog on the same afternoon, the track looks to be in much smarter condition. Hunslet diesel *Weightin* is waiting, while one of the crew attends to some matter at the far end and Barclay WHR2 has its driver in place, ready for the next stage in the day's work. The membrane newly laid under the track, to help hold it in place, protrudes from beneath the ballast in the foreground. *Cliff Thomas*

We now approach the railway's famous 'flat crossing' of the ex-Cambrian Railways standard-gauge line. In the seven decades since the lifting of the WHR track, the alignment has been in use as a footpath, with, initially, an A-frame set of steps over the boundary fence and a foot crossing over the 'main line'. By 3 June 2003 this arrangement has been dispensed with and the sign points right, denoting the diversion to a more formal crossing a few yards further on. The undergrowth makes it hard to imagine there ever having been room for a railway here. The base of a water tower can just be seen beyond, covered in ivy, in this view towards the town.

By 30 October 2006, with early preparations for reinstatement of the crossing under way, even that diversion has been lost and walkers are no longer allowed beyond the mesh fencing. The water tower base is more easily seen here and is a poignant and remarkable survivor of the old railway. The site is now officially known as Cae Pawb, and Network Rail's standard-gauge line is immediately beyond the fence; this view shows some of the challenges facing the new railway.

Just three days later the transformation is dramatic. Standard-gauge track panels have been lifted from both sides of the crossing, the bed on both railways prepared, a pre-formed crossing lowered into place and the track panels renewed, ready for reinstatement of 'main-line' running just a few days later. Much more work has to be done, however, before the new WHR can be joined up on either side of the crossing.

Crossing to the other side of the Network Rail line we look back at the former footpath on 30 October 2006 (*left*), immediately before the contractor's attentions were turned in this direction. Fenced off and submerged beneath prodigious undergrowth, it seems unlikely that this was ever a railway route!

Just one day later (*above*) the transition is astounding! Today's hydraulically powered machines can work wonders in hours that would have taken mere manpower several days, and this is the situation just 29 hours after the first photograph. The standard-gauge track panels have been lifted, ballast removed and the alignment of both railways is attacked with gusto by the Komatsu PC128US tracked road/rail machine.

After a further four or five hours of work, into the morning of 1 November, the progress is impressive and self-evident. These three happy 'monkeys' are more likely to be 'feel no fingers' as they manoeuvre the three Whacker compactors over the freshly laid ballast, vibrating it into a smooth bed ready for the track. Notice how, now that the undergrowth has been cleared, there appears to be much more space for the railway!

Less than three hours after the third shot on the previous page, all is in readiness for the installation of the actual flat crossing in the early afternoon of 1 November 2006. In true *Blue Peter* style, the crossing is one that had been 'prepared earlier'; the huge crane gently lowers the mix of narrow and standard gauge, with the 'man on the ground' holding the rope to ensure that the gauges are placed in their proper alignment. There was much excitement amongst the spectators as the assembly approached its resting place.

Less than 24 hours later, in the late morning of 2 November, rails are again in place on the standard gauge, while the narrow-gauge route awaits further attention at some later date. There is no time to stand around and watch now, as all stops are pulled out to finalise the job, ready for service trains on the main line to restart within three days.

Two hours later ballast is being dropped strategically in place and the whole is beginning to look like a fully functional railway once more. On this occasion, the narrowness of the gauge being unfamiliar, the skills of the supervisor and, especially, the road/rail machine driver were brilliantly exhibited. Notice the old track now joined up to the new section on the right.

Finally, we come to a rare and unrepeatable shot – the first traffic across the installation! At precisely 1644 and 50 seconds on 1 November 2006, prior to any ballast being laid in place, one of BCL's PW150ES road/rail machines is captured as it gingerly crawls across the new crossing, carefully watched by supervisors. While the beginning of the works had been in rain and fast drizzle, the final couple of days saw perfect weather with, on this occasion, the lowering late autumn sunshine delightfully picking out the tableau and helping to raise everyone's spirits as the end of the task was in sight.

Left With the abandonment of the line into Porthmadog after 1937, the trackbed was initially enjoyed by walkers, but after the subsequent re-routing of the path, as we have already seen, nature had a free hand and went wild! Thus on 3 June 2003 Porthmadog's version of the Amazon jungle comprises rampant brambles amongst other greenery, making it almost impassable. The old water tower base is in the centre distance, with the site of the earlier flat crossing beyond and the roofs of Gelert's Farm buildings to the left.

   Almost inconceivably this is the same location, as the water tower and the outline of the hills in the background (albeit tinged with mist on this later date) confirm. On 26 January 2008 progress has reached the site of the former Portmadoc New station and has created order out of chaos. The trackbed has been levelled, supported on either side with gabions of rock, and membrane and ballast have been laid ready for track to be installed some six months or so later. The neighbouring sites have also changed dramatically over the five years since the earlier view.

This page By 4 August 2008 wooden sleepers are in place and the prefabricated 'wide to gauge' trap point is on site, with discussion under way as to the final positioning of the panel. We are looking towards the town, with the site of the original Portmadoc New station immediately beyond the water tower, and the station building on a lower level to the right, on the site now occupied by the builder's materials.

   Track needs to be securely fixed to the sleepers, whether as plain line or, as here, a more complicated arrangement. Once again, the modern way is far more powerful and speedier than by manpower alone. Looking towards the flat crossing on the same day as above, bolts are tightened on the trap point panel.

Leaving the site of Cae Pawb and Portmadoc New, the new railway has another crossing to negotiate, at Snowdon Street. As seen on 26 January 2008, the street is ahead, with the Snowdon Flour Mill to the left, as clearance of the route gets under way. Yet more new fencing is in place on the left, alongside another stretch of rock gabion and membrane.

A little short of three months later, on 14 April, the course of the railway is now plain to see (*below*). Tramway-style track has been laid upon a concrete base, with metal spurs in place to help strengthen the infilling of further concrete that is to come. The tight curve of the route into the town is apparent from this angle; the sight of a Garratt approaching round the bend will be something to be savoured once the railway opens!

By 4 August (*above right*) the approach to Snowdon Street has been completed, with the rails set in their concrete bed and the area smartened. Ahead is the final stretch of the Cross Town Link, and exactly the same method will be used across Britannia Bridge.

Swinging round through 180 degrees on the same day (*below*), the extent of tracklaying towards Cae Pawb is seen, as is the rebuilding of the bridge over Y Cyt, which leaves the Afon Glaslyn near the harbour entrance. The original pillars have been utilised, but clothed in new slate, while the main part of the bridge has been very smartly rebuilt. Note the transition from tramway to standard rail at this point.

Across Snowdon Street on 26 January 2008, the gaping hole in the new trackbed alignment exemplifies the scale of works required to return the rails to Porthmadog. The ageing pipe here uncovered will be protected by concrete within the wooden shuttering, to support the track and trains in due course. As will be seen by comparison with old photographs, the two houses beyond the street and the mountains in the distance have changed very little over the years.

By 4 August 2008 the preparations have been completed and the trackbed is in the final stages of construction, with rails now running across Snowdon Street. A stack of new wooden sleepers awaits use, while beyond construction employees discuss some matter.

And so we reach the High Street on 26 January 2008, where Britannia Bridge crosses the Afon Glaslyn. Preparations are under way to bring the railway across High Street, and will involve removing part of the bridge parapet to allow some easing of the curved entrance to the road. Work will also be needed on part of the riverbank and the trilby-hatted gentleman seen on the right is peering at that area while the large crane waits for its next lift.

Just three months later, on 28 April, the bank underpinning is nearing completion and the necessary length of parapet has been removed. Preparation of the trackbed is the next task, together with a footpath to allow pedestrians to once again stroll along the side of the river and onto the bridge; a short stretch of this path can be seen already in situ. Left of centre, work is under way to convert the old Co-op building into a Wilkinson's store.

Above This is not an unusual scene on the A487 as it approaches the town centre from the east, especially in summer, as tourists and holidaymakers head along the High Street. Signs of recent developments on 4 August 2008 are, however, not hard to spot. The truncated parapet is seen on the left, the angled wall providing greater allowance for the trains, and there are tracks set in the roadway. Snaking across the bridge – not following the exact trajectory of the original WHR – they now await completion of the Cross Town Link and the arrival of test trains before opening in 2009. Note, also, the pyramid cobbles, warning pedestrians of the presence of the railway.

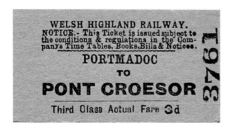

Right Here is another view demonstrating that rebuilding a railway is much more than merely placing track on the ground! The minefield of logistics and many months of planning – and obtaining permission to disrupt traffic – have all been painstakingly negotiated before anything can be done, but now the work has begun. On 14 April 2008, before the holiday season gets into full swing, one side of the road, on the approach to the FR's Harbour station, has been coned off, dug up and rails put in place. At this time the sinuous curve seems to be misaligned, but a reverse curve and removal of a few feet of the Cob Records warehouse (seen just past the excavator) will make the necessary adjustment.

Exactly 14 days later, on 28 April, this side of the road has been restored to something like normality, while the other carriageway is now occupied, but this time by what appears to be the Gas Board. Note that the entrance to the local housing and the FR's car park, to the right, has been adjusted to accommodate the new railway.

123

In this portrait of Britannia Bridge the road is eerily quiet. On 1 May 2004 the proposed changes are still in the future and this perspective, looking into the town from the FR's station, is largely unchanged from the previous two or three decades. The Cross Town Link is still a pipe dream at this juncture, with many within the town not wholly in support – and many enthusiasts not daring to believe it could happen! – reinforcing yet again how much time and effort those behind the new WHR have had to expend to realise their goals.

The same aspect on 7 September 2008 shows that not only have rails been laid over the bridge and across the road, but also how unobtrusive the result is, the rails being embedded in concrete. Other than the occasional appearance of a train and yellow road markings delineating the railway, it is quite conceivable that many motorists will not even be aware that they are driving over an iron road. In the foreground, realignment of the exit road from the Snowdon Wharf residential dwellings and the FR car park is the only major change.

The final destination: from 2009 the FR's Harbour station will once again be joined to the WHR, with this last stretch running into the station through where the left-hand car stands in this view from 26 January 2008. To reach that point, from the reverse curves from the river bridge, some 3 metres will be sliced from the Cob Records warehouse, seen on the right, with the notice of forthcoming demolition on display. With a new platform installed for WHR travellers adjacent to the FR's 'Spooner's' café/restaurant/bar (seen between the four vehicles), there should be a ready trade for refreshment of throat and palate!

The slightly wider angle, a little over six months later on 4 August 2008, shows the new railway sweeping into the station complex, with the truncation at this end of the Cob Records store being compensated by an extension at the right-hand end; the difference in roof levels shows the new addition. Again, the yellow clearance dots on the road mark out the width needed for the trains to run unheeded. An FR train stands on the existing track; this will eventually be realigned to allow for the creation of the new WHR platform.

Above Another view from 4 August 2008 shows just how close the new railway has come to its final destination by this date. Just beyond 'Spooner's', behind the row of seats, a white concrete strip marks out the edge of the proposed platform area; this will be extended to accommodate the lengthy trains that will sweep down from the mountains. The need to realign the FR platform track can be judged from this angle, as FR trains waiting to transport WHR passengers onwards will not wish to block access for the new arrivals.

Above right Looking back towards the vantage point of the picture opposite on 7 September 2008, the current proximity of the FR and WHR tracks can be judged, even though the final installation has not yet been achieved. The 'temporary engineering connection', laid in February 2008, remains in the foreground, and this will no doubt serve for the early days of the new connection, to be replaced at a later date. Happily, however, apart from the new platform and some realignment of the FR's existing track, the ambience of Harbour station, much loved over the years, should not be too adversely affected.

Right ...and finally! Part of the appeal of the resurgent WHR is the mouthwatering prospect of the ex-South African Garratts working hard through the Aberglaslyn Pass. The railway is well aware of this appeal and the need to have sufficient Garratts in service at any one time. To this end, No 87 is the latest to be added to the roster and is seen here on its first outing across the Cob, in January 2009. Looking almost as if it had just come off a train from the Welsh Highland rails, it stands just out of Harbour station, with the station buildings and the turnout to the WHR in the background. *Roger Dimmick*

INDEX